LEAVING ONE'S COMFORT ZONE

The Story of a Move to Italy

LEAVING ONE'S COMFORT ZONE
The Story of a Move to Italy

Gökhan Kutluer

TRANSNATIONAL PRESS LONDON

2021

TRANSNATIONAL LIVES: 3

LEAVING ONE'S COMFORT ZONE

The Story of a Move to Italy

Gökhan Kutluer

Copyright © 2021 Transnational Press London

All rights reserved. This book or any portion thereof may not be reproduced or used in any manner whatsoever without the express written permission of the publisher except for the use of brief quotations in a book review or scholarly journal.

First Published in 2021 by TRANSNATIONAL PRESS LONDON in the United Kingdom, 12 Ridgeway Gardens, London, N6 5XR, UK.
www.tplondon.com

Transnational Press London® and the logo and its affiliated brands are registered trademarks.

Requests for permission to reproduce material from this work should be sent to: sales@tplondon.com

Paperback
ISBN: 978-1-80135-057-0
Digital
ISBN: 978-1-80135-058-7

Cover Design: Mert Göker
Translation: İrem Bilkin
Editor: Elif Naz Güveniş
Contributors: Dilara Ararat, Melis Aktaş, Verena Scola and The British Guy

Transnational Press London Ltd. is a company registered in England and Wales No. 8771684.

To my family and to the woman who calls me "my soul"…

CONTENTS

CONTENTS 1
ABOUT THE AUTHOR 2
EDITOR'S NOTE 3
PREFACE 5

CHAPTER I STORY 8
    General Trajectory 9
    Freud's Chair 23
    Target Locked 28
    Final Hours 33
    First Siege of Bergamo 37
    Job Hunting in Italy 47
    I Will Be Back 54
    Montenegro Adventure 62
    Second Siege of Bergamo 72

CHAPTER II IMPRESSIONS OF ITALY 93
    Life In Italy 95
    About Being an Expat 103
    Epilogue 108

CHAPTER III DIARY 109

ABOUT THE AUTHOR

Gökhan Kutluer was born January 25, 1986, and raised in Istanbul at a time. Playing in one's neighborhood with friends was still pure fun at the time. Gökhan first attended Taş Private Elementary School, and then Cağaloğlu Anatolian High School, one of the oldest and internationally renowned high schools of Turkey. He went on to study Political Science and International Relations at Bahçeşehir University. He focused on writing travel articles for magazines as well as working on his own blog after receiving his BA. This path led him to what initially started as a hobby, then turned into a passion and, naturally, a profession around bicycles. With this in mind, he became the senior editor at Cyclist, a monthly magazine in Turkey.

Kutluer aims to enhance his expertise in the cycling world and devotes himself to building recognition in this area by blending the cultural and athletic aspects of cycling. The draft of his first book, Cloud Factory (Bulut Fabrikası), which is currently being translated into English, appeared while Gökhan was unable to resist the urge to move to Italy; a crave embarked itself on him ever since he set foot on Italian soil during his undergraduate Erasmus days. The move to Bergamo, Italy, was a turning point marked by Cloud Factory having been both published and adapted into a theatre play.

Leaving One's Comfort Zone - The Story of a Move to Italy, his second book, followed no later than a year while Gökhan was in the process of completing his third year in Italy.

In his seventh year abroad, Gökhan currently divides his time between Rome and Berlin writing independently for travel magazines and working as a digital marketer.

EDITOR'S NOTE

Since the mid-2000's, "Leaving Turkey" has been a social phenomenon associated with the changing social atmosphere, declining economy (more so in the last few years) and a fear that is associated with state power/violence... Compared to the migration from other Middle Eastern or Post-Colonial African or Asian Countries, the phenomena of "Leaving Turkey" has emerged from and is almost, only contained to the well-educated middle, upper-middle class who holds the idea of not belonging, not seeing a future in well harmony with their own ideologies...

As it is still an ongoing phenomenon, there aren't much literary or artistic representations that contribute to this reality. I, myself, am also a Kennismigrant as they call it in Dutch. For these reasons and my own, I believe Gökhan's novel not only presents as a migrant, auto-fiction literary text; it also engages with this social problem of brain drain from Turkey.

Gökhan addresses a whole generation of well-educated, middle or upper-middle class wanting to leave Turkey, even though remaining subjective and auto-fictional. His engagement with this social problem is hidden in the first chapters of Leaving One's Comfort Zone. It is not a coincidence that this novel's Turkish reception was a success. There are a few, in our generations, who have narrated their story of leaving Turkey due to its social chaos.

Kutluer gives voice to a social problem that has drastically increased in the last five years, long after Kutluer has left his own comfort zone. From Taş Koleji to Cağaloğlu High School, presumably offered "a good education" which somewhat means "Western values embedded in modern ethics" in Istanbul. Evidently, this is my subjective claim and translation which is open to refutation. As is depicted in the first chapter, Gökhan leaves Turkey to take a distance with the never-ending social battles Turkey faces. A feeling of being home; but feeling like an immigrant at home. It is the feeling that stems "I am from this society; I belong to this society; but maybe not that much."

As his migrant reality, sinks in, another battle starts. All these struggles add up to present itself almost like Bildungsroman. A privileged, maybe not very satisfied but adventurous soul going on a journey to part from family, from society, from pain to build a life, one might say. Thus, these are all the aspects that make this auto-fictional limpid and clear to engage with.

Edward Said once claimed "beyond the frontier between 'us' and 'the outsiders' is the perilous territory of understanding". My generation of people who grew up in Turkey, as well as Gökhan's, struggle to find a new breathing space out of a land that stems from a distorted sense of "us." Kutluer compares and contrasts his Turkish roots, his old social surroundings to his new encounters in Bergamo and Montenegro. Starting from the relief of "getting out," he dwells with the deep sense of nostalgia, the inevitable feeling of exile and loneliness; yet knowing that going back is not always an option and it is not the same land that one goes back to. Echoing some Turkish-German literature like Emine Sevgi Özdamar, Güney Dal, Feridun Zaimoğlu he battles the layers of integration to a new environment in reflection to his feelings of what once was a home to its aftertaste.

These examples I have given have a different experience of being Gasterbeiters in the 1950's and 1960's. It proves the scarcity of literary and artistic production on Turkey's current brain drain, having found these examples. I am proud to have been a small part of Gökhan's journey, travelling with him by editing his sentences, experiences while reflecting on my own. My hope is to come across other literary works that engage with the aforementioned social phenomena, and our million-year-old reality which is migrating..

Elif Naz

PREFACE

"Any settlers in the family?"

"You don't look Turkish at all, are you an émigré?"

"Where are you originally from?"

From an early age, I started hearing these questions. Either in school, during a cab ride, in the office or in my new social circles. I face these questions right after we start chatting... and this happens often.

I always expect it.

"Gökhan, where are you from?"

I evolved: my height, my features, my voice, my gestures, the way I think, and many more but the answer to this question has never changed:

"My ancestors used to live in Greece. They were there for a few generations. With the convention concerning population exchange between Turkey and Greece, my ancestors moved here permanently."

What I kept hearing on the grapevine eventually became a solid truth. I came to grasp the fact that my ancestors lived in Drama, Ptolemaida and Eleftheroupoli in Greece.

All this longing to flee from my homeland and desire to get to know other places would clearly relate to a genetic interpretation. However, I still couldn't say it all fit.

How much of what took place during the population exchange could be volitional? Who knows how many families were implicitly relocated and merely thrown into other people's lives? Doesn't it appear to be grim for those who used to live in contentment to leave so much behind?

When it comes to my grandparents I am at a loss to conceive certain facts. I believe.. perhaps they were extremely enthusiastic about starting anew.

As I've stated, I am not certain. Willing or not, all my descents were émigrés. It would be proper for me to state that in my family, there is no generation that was born in the city. More or less, this fact shaped my approach to my current status. "Aha! It runs in the family," I've said to myself. I pay less attention to this issue.

***

At university I was particularly interested in two subject areas which were related to what I was studying. Contextually, I am content to be left to my own devices. I enrolled myself in International Migration and Introduction to Social Psychology. My international migration lecturer was Sema Erder, a well-known name in terms of migration studies. Her work consisted of immigrants in Turkey.

I got goosebumps each lesson when Professor Erder asked us a question. Her questions were nourished with immense knowledge on internal and external immigration:

"What type of experience, do you think, would make an individual consider leaving the country one was born and brought up in? Whose language they spoke? Where they had friends and knew every corner by heart?"

She was asking this question on our first day at the faculty as a mental exercise. However, I clearly remember the sensation of feeling like hitting a wall hearing the question.. I was taken aback by such a question for the simplest reason. After spending a whole semester in Italy, I felt unhappy during the next semester back in Turkey.

On the one hand, my university offered classes on subjects that I adored. On the other, there were classes that I disliked… While I was juggling between courses, I grew a sensation to the distortions Istanbul lay ahead. I saw and observed things in a distinctive manner.

Every Erasmus student from Turkey faces a culture shock on their return home. So did I. The return wounded me. My desire to travel, what could initially be defined as mere curiosity evolved into a desire to flee Turkey, especially now. It is not a mere coincidence that I was attracted by a course on migration and the questions that were tied to it.

***

Leaving One's Comfort Zone is the outcome of a major milestone in my twenties. During that decade, the desire to flee Turkey grew in me. By this publication, I intend to reach out for those who need a guidebook in emigrating from their home. Keep in mind, my experience is subjective, like any other. Not everyone experiences a similar journey, not each migrant's path looks like one another. Not every Turkish citizen would make this choice. Leaving Turkey relies on my free will. The painstakingly drifting path I took resembles a crow which blindly follows as a guide.

CHAPTER I

STORY

GENERAL TRAJECTORY

Presumably, the decision to leave one's homeland is a phenomenon which demands reassessment. It is a multidimensional process. Only after completing the assessment of your mental and physical capacity; can you be ready for departure. If you're unaccustomed to the idea of "leaving", you end up more unhinged and frail than expected. It makes it harder to commence the destination against the challenges that lie ahead.

In such a case, you might start dreaming of going back at the first opportunity that arises. A solid foundation for departure is a must. This indicates a demand for reassurance and determination. You should get used to the idea of flying on a plane. Your mindset should be in top form, you should be prepared to provide consistent answers to the possible reactions raised around you. The most important thing is to learn to trust your skills.

Never forget that you're not only made up of the education that rendered you to become a perfect consumer. You also carry your family's ethical contribution, your cultural and communal practices and above all, the voice of your inner child.

Once the idea of departure arises, it will not be possible to push it away. At least this was how I experienced it. When you cannot see beyond the massive sphere that holds everything; from the perspective of family, of your social environment and of your relationships to your quality of life you start feeling depressed. That's the right time to move away.

***

Things were a bit complicated when I was born. My father was a dedicated working-class guy who spent his years in a well-known company. My mother was an orphan who devoted her whole life to us, her family.

My parents lost my baby sister Nagihan before I was born. My nuclear family was even more shaken and desolate by Nihan's diagnosis with epilepsy. This was right before my birth. The family had to endure the financial and the emotional repercussions Nihan's condition caused. While they were taking care of my sister while raising me in the midst of the Chernobyl disaster. Chernobyl happened three months after I was born. Medical visitation and practice were scarce. Plus, medications were sought after.

I was only eleven. A 5th grader, about to take the middle school entrance exam when we lost my elder sister. She didn't get to call my name. Nor could we recollect any childhood memories. For instance, any that resembles us acting as double trouble and or us misbehaving. As the critical early childhood years had already passed; detaching from my mother to find a replacement role model became emotionally problematic to me.

It was as though my family and I were all in a screenplay and I was the one dealing with parents who were a nervous wreck, even though they had every right to be so. Strangely enough, I looked very happy in my primary school graduation photos posing with the veteran actor Tarık Akan. He was the founder of Taş Private Elementary School and was known well for his ongoing support for the working class. I shamed my father, who was never satisfied with my grades during my academic life, a tad bit when I managed to enter a well known public middle school. Just a little bit though.. because I couldn't get into the number one prestigious school and I was only waitlisted for the second-best option.

My score was sufficient enough to enroll in many Turkish private schools except for the first top few. I remember very well that I really wanted to get into one of the private French Schools or the Italian School. However, after investing the majority of his budget on my sister's treatment, my father enrolled me into Cağaloğlu Anatolian High School. It was the third best option among the elite public schools back then, to eliminate the financial risks.

I was eleven. Since "I wasn't at an age able to comprehend any of this process", my father went ahead and made the decision for me. Such bullocks of an education system!

I remember the day of the school tour, just before I enrolled. It was like yesterday. The school building was in good shape; but, still, neglected. Each footstep I made caused a creaking noise.

High ceilings, big, slim doors with dated polish, a neglected garden, a basketball court with barely their visible lines and a canteen that reeked of cooking oil.

Gökhan who attended a private elementary school had to experience public school. He used to play the organ and the piano in music lessons and whose teacher was convinced he had talent. Aside from what went on in our family, this was pretty much my first trauma. I walked through the school. Checked out the classrooms and the toilets. Those were huge disappointments. I was in denial about Turkish Republic's facts. I had to face them. To observe the impacts of its economical power on its people as well as on its education system.

***

During the first year of high school, the primary languages of instruction were German and Turkish. I had a good start at German prep class. I would help out my classmates in their difficulties of understanding certain things. This way I was also able to practise. I trusted myself to learn German.

I was also about to fall hard for the petite, blonde who sat at the desk in front of me.

Both our desks were by the window. Until lunchtime, the rays of sun were reflected from her goldie locks. I was extremely distracted by her.

However, everything went south. Learning German felt like acquiring the Chinese language as I fell ill with thalassemia. I was away from school a lot in the first semester. It was a breaking point and from then on: I completely lost track of the grasp of the language. Neither private tutors nor individual efforts helped me catch my classmates' level. I was alienated by everything and everyone affiliated with Cağaloğlu.

As I detached from German, I also inevitably detached from the school curriculum. The failed attempts of learning German were pretty tiring. Especially since, I was disinterested in learning science in German. I was being disobedient in class, getting told off by my biology teacher who nicknamed me "Faule Socke!" as I was constantly cheating in exams. I barely made it to the next year thanks to the teachers' committee verdicts.

My damaged relationship with my dad, who religiously took hold of the computer cable; my computer altogether after my shitty report cards, earned me a lousy habit of not being able to sit at dinner tables at great length. This was also the cause of a relentless scrutiny by almost all the women who entered my life and found out that I was restless at dinner tables. Each family dinner started to fuel a troublesome discussion regarding my low performance at school. The discussions revolved around my irresponsibility, to the chagrin of my parents, I would sit the dinner late, eat in a hurry and be excused.

I was beginning to feel as if I didn't belong to that school any longer. It was pointless to do any work. I thought love could save me. Conversely, I lost hope in that direction as well after a few failed relationships, platonic or else.

Friendships I made were sometimes good and sometimes not so good. It never reached a point where I had to end a friendship. At least we had football. I loved goalkeeping. I loved the task of goalkeeping. My friend Safa, on the other hand, liked to defend the goalpost only because he would be in the shade, away from the sunlight.

It was fun to watch the game from there. I enjoyed giving commands to my teammates for defence. Football managing games interested me at that time. I was generally a good goalie, though every now and then we lost a score because of my silly behavior. If my friends sensed that I was not in the mood they knew the drill. They would tell me so when the girl(s), whoever I'd fancy then, would be watching the game. It took me seeing a girl I fancied to play like Peter Schmeichel.

Good old times!

***

I took the school service bus for seven years including the prep year. School services were a thing in Istanbul during my youth. The city is huge and not the safest place. Many people commute. My parents found the courage to visit Nihan's grave after she passed away. The weekly visits consisted of leaving flowers at her grave. Whereas I spent a minimum of two hours commuting to school and back for seven years. I kept commuting back and forth to a place I hardly preferred to be. My head used to be full of thoughts during my highschool years.

The bosphorus of Istanbul consists of a kilometers long, coastal road. I used that road to commute to my school. Eventually, what is beautiful to tourists became a dislike for me.

The hardships I had to deal with when learning German language was substituted with the university exam, which each Turkish citizen has to take to enter into a University. Even though I felt the burden of the university entrance exam on my shoulders, which consisted of me learning basic science, did not ease its way to the subject.

Since my educational foundation wasn't strong enough, I got low grades from maths and physics. I wasn't really interested in the knowledge. I chose TM in 10th grade. In Turkish educational system students could choose either Turkish/Math, Science or Turkish/Social Studies. These three categories, subject areas students had to choose in the second year in highschool, defined the University exams they were going to get ready for as well.

I failed in Turkish/Math; couldn't get hold of the mandatory math and geometry lectures. It was obvious this whole thing was going to be a pain and here was the proof. I was denied my diploma, in my senior year, due to my failed grades in math and geometry. This meant I couldn't enroll in Yeditepe University's Tourism and Hotel Management school. Yeditepe is one of the acknowledged, old universities in Istanbul. Courses are taught in English in Yeditepe.

Nevertheless, I did not study enough for the university exam as much as I should have.

I was tutored by my primary school teacher's son. He now lives on the other side of the world. With his contribution, I passed my failed math and geometry courses the following winter. Thus, I graduated. After retaking the university exam, I managed to get into Bahçeşehir University Political Science and International Relations school receiving more or less the same score as the year before. Bahçeşehir is also one of the English-taught, now acknowledged, private universities in Istanbul.

As one got their exam results, they would make five choices of university remplacements. I don't remember my exact placement but my top choices were law faculties of various colleges. I was sure of my success, it should have been a high achiever. Some of my friends had matriculated at prestigious universities. My parents compared theory success to mine. They scrutinized me for not being as successful. However, this situation didn't stop me and my parents from enrolling me at a university.

Studying Political Science and International Relations was pretty popular at the time, in Turkey. I don't know why; but men in suits working at newspapers or publishing supplements couldn't recommend these faculties enough. Especially in their columns in those years. They went on emphasizing how much the graduates of these schools would be needed in the future's global world. Currently, I think that university education is not a predicate for a profession.

On the other hand, in terms of personal growth and self involvement the school offers a lot. With the premise of a solid foundation or with hunger for knowledge, this school feeds curiosity and lets you grow. On the contrary, if you did nothing up until university or if you're enrolled in there just for the sake of it, the analogy I'd use to define the experience would be a book sitting on a dusty shelf.

If you don't have any interest in art, history, movies, plays, literature; no prior knowledge of literary classics and are not curious about an author, this department is not for you. Even though you indulge yourself in Eastern philosophy, read self growth books or finish schools, you can't catch up.

In short, it is possible to gain alternative perspectives through various case analyses by studying at this school. Unfortunately, Political Sciences won't grant you a proper profession. It's alright if you'd like to be an academic. However, if you're unsure about which direction to take in order to have a job, you have a tough task ahead. Any plans to step into politics? Then, be prepared to be tormented since true politics is a lot more complex than presumed. .

***

I hold immense appreciation for my parents. They made it possible for me to complete five years at university. Including the prep year, I managed to finish school by only concentrating on the subjects that I really liked. My parents, during this time, sold some of their stuff, moved into a smaller place and took out bank loans to provide me with a good academic life. At some point I was about to fail at statistics and economics, even did so one term. I finally got it all together. There were times in which, during the exam, I was unable to reach a final answer even though I had all the information. I never excelled at calculation.

I used to love Political Ideologies and History of Political Thought courses. I would meticulously take notes in the subjects of political behavior, leadership, philosophy, international migration, history of diplomacy, introduction to psychology and social psychology. I scanned my notes and used to email them to my classmates. Never was I a student who'd be secretive about his notes or one who'd make profit out of them. But, while saying that, my hatred toward those few mates who were reluctant to share course notes for subjects I disliked is still raw.

I held a strong dislike to some of the courses. One that I disliked and received low grades was literary studies. I believe my low grade was due to the course's content or the lecturer. I had classmates who had difficulty with Turkish grammar. Nevertheless, we were all responsible for submitting assignments on a few, boring books.

When I came across questions in final exams (that were also considered as midterms); I made comments and criticized the exam harshly on the exam paper. In my answers, I wrote how much of a pain it was to stick to a curriculum. One that is utterly meaningless. The fact that I had not submitted any answers; but, passed the exam was proof that I was right. Throughout the semester I never even once looked at the teacher. She gave me a pass. Now I knew I wouldn't see her again. Funny enough, by giving me a passing grade -without criticising my inappropriate exam sheet- she showed her own color.

***

As a family, we were not in the habit of moving house a lot. Since I needed more opportunities so I could experience more of life, it was truly a breaking point for me when it happened, to be able to go to Italy on a scholarship for a half-term on the Erasmus exchange program. I should point out that I reached that breaking point analyzing myself in the following years rather than dealing with it whilst going through it. In other words, it is correct to say, it took me some time to realize the effects of the role it played on my character as a person who never set foot on foreign soil before but now lived in a small medieval Italian city.

The move to Siena after a cosmopolitan city such as Istanbul was an outstanding experience. I collected many memories in this cute and touristic city. To witness the slow living in Italy's charming streets, to be in communication with lots of individuals from all walks of life, to play football, to get wasted at nights and visit other Italian towns made me begin to develop a kinship to Italy. That was more than adequate for me to acknowledge that there was a life elsewhere and it was possible to hope.

One evening at a dinner everybody was chatting about what they'd be doing next once their school finished. Some friends said they were going to indulge in traveling around the world and then see what would come next while others said they would be taking a long vacation. One even expressed their will to purchase a caravan and drive around every single corner in Europe. They were free to move about and travel since they were EU passport holders. When it was my turn to tell them about my plans, I realized I didn't have much to share because I hadn't asked that question to myself. Alas, there was a sad fact wholeheartedly embraced in Turkey: immediately after one graduated s(he) would get a job. Otherwise, everybody's main concern would be, "So, your son finished school, now what?... or when is he going to start work?" The interrogation would never end.

I spent the last few weeks of the remaining academic year visiting some European cities only to return home crying my eyes out. Istanbul is such an awkward place… it didn't take more than a few days to become entangled into its rhythm and rot in its own abyss. All of a sudden I found myself tense again among the crowds who paced the earth rapidly. And because I was brought up and always been taught to catch up, I automatically started acting like I was one of them. There was no trace of the calm Gökhan of a few weeks prior.

Shortly after I returned home the second semester began and the first class was with my all time favourite professor İlkay Sunar's. He talked about Renaissance and Florence; even mentioned Machiavelli whose statue I posed next to just a month ago. It was like seeing the girlfriend I had broken up with who I was still in love with. Italy kept creeping up on me the more I tried to forget about it and it took me a while to acknowledge that I should learn to live with its memories.

***

Senior students at university were in the habit of asking one another what they'd be doing next. Some were chasing after internships, some were going to start working in family businesses. There were some who would only frequent cafes. Others, like myself, watched chaos from a distance... We were a strange bunch and just as Tony Montana said, none of us had an instinct regarding who we wanted to become.

It wasn't long before I sent my resume to one of the headhunters via school's reference. I started a paid internship at an international logistics company. It was a pretty showoff back then; because, none of my classmates were working on a salary. After gaining some experience for a few months, I graduated. There was six months between my graduation and my first job. It was foolish to start a job right after I graduated. I got promoted twice in my first six months at work. Additionally, I had a fortnight vacation abroad and became convinced that most of my colleagues were dull, including my boss.

In the end, I was sacked. The following months were a nightmare. My parents kept pestering me, "Have we wasted our means?" on the verge of me being sacked. Luckily, I got hired in another job. A few months passed before I decided to ignore my military service deferment and started my service two years earlier than scheduled. This was an exceptional experience. In approximately five months, without a break, I served both in Kastamonu and Erzincan. Kastamonu is a small city in the black sea region. Erzincan is another small one in the east with a big Kurdish population. My experience in Erzincan was a genuine eye-opener in facing certain social facts about Turkey, which were at distance. I demonstrated a stunning performance in rifle training despite my frail constitution in Kastamonu. I was granted a day's leave due to my success in rifle training. That gave me a smile.

My military service was completed without any breaks involving the bootcamp and cadetship. I didn't understand why I was so reluctant to finish it right away. Psychologically, I must have had a substantial motive in completing my tasks. School, employment, military service. "Check. Check. Check. What's next?" A constant wave of packaged deals, lists of objectives that are done one by one... I made peace with the notion that I was one of those kids who acted like a racing horse. Finally I started a new job with the help of a guy I met during my service who I'm still in contact with.

Depression hit when I entered my professional life. I was well aware that there were excuses such as finishing military service this time. Constant telltale, playing up behind everyone's backs, using a high-pitched voice while pacing around the boss' office -so he could hear how hardworking they all are- grappling with which degree and mode the AC should best be on... I hung in there for fifteen months. My soul was drained. I did not quit my job because I had purchased a city bicycle. I started commuting from Sefaköy to the office in Zincirlikuyu (30 km in distance). In other words, I was crossing one side of Istanbul to the other by bike, which made my colleagues believe I was mad. Zincirlikuyu is the financial center of Istanbul. In short, I had spent all my money on the bike, maxed out my credit cards, thus I had to work.

***

Although I did not study tourism, this was now my field of employment. Tourism does have a lot of glitches despite the fact that it looks like it involves a lot of fun. The hardest part for me was while I was assisting and directing people to all corners in the world for their travels, I had to stay behind a desk in doing so. It hurt looking at a screen revealing many countries and cities and dreaming about them. In order to overcome this state, I started spending more time riding my bike. Now I commuted to work on my bike every day and found myself dreaming riding elsewhere, as well. Soon enough I paired with a friend, Burak, and upon his offer, we ended up in Scandinavia for a bike tour that lasted ten days stretching from Oslo to Copenhagen.

It was during this tour that I realized riding a bike really touched my soul. Burak was a little tired one day so he decided to take a train to our next destination. I rode my bike. A hundred kilometers of riding buried me in my thoughts. The experience resembled the deep continuity of newspapers being printed consequently in a printing house. Ideas forming, sensations flowing and me witnessing a unique geography lying ahead.. all got intermingled. What transpired from my eyes or into my mind was all it took to keep me on track. However, what kept my integration intact was not the bicycle itself. I merged with my boyhood again, things touching his heart. For instance, my inner child was determined to talk to his childhood love, on the bike. It was a moment of mindfulness where I discovered I still had the power to transform my life.

One of the partners at the firm tried to convince me towards accepting the current economic system. Despite my respect to him, they were failed attempts. I stopped having any future prospect about myself in that office. I sold my bike, upgraded to a roadster once I was back from a tour. I compulsively began visiting forums and shopping websites and, eventually, shopping in light of my newly attained knowledge.

Being in office was a phase, it was not a necessity. As that comprehension sunk in, I quit. However, due to workload at the office, combined with my boss regarding me as out of my mind, my resignation was rescinded. It still didn't work out. I ruined a daily tour of a group of Art History students from New Zealand. I could no longer work at my job. That gave me joy.

***

I spent my initial salaries on informal clothing. I spent a big portion on any extension regarding bikes. The final stages of my corporate life were spent in contemplation. It all coincided with the tear gas and water cannons firing at protesters from the TOMA trucks when the Gezi Park events, protests were happening in 2013.

I discussed these protests in my first book The Cloud Factory. Gezi Events did not particularly score a colossal political accomplishment in the country's near future. Yet, the events were immensely impactful in their own right; I was to make my own radical change.

Regardless of the power and energy Gezi events gave me, I quit my job. I wrote an email which then I sent to eight separate email addresses in various id combinations. Their recipients were company managers I had heard of:

Hello Mr. Uzunhasan,

First, I shall shortly introduce myself and explain why I am sending you this email. I have a BA degree, completed my military service and possess an advanced level of English. I also have overseas experience from travelling abroad. Exactly a year ago, I got myself tangled with the love of bicycles after purchasing a Specialized Sirrus from your shop. Ever since then, I have observed quite a lot of changes I wanted to affect in my life. The tours I've been to really boosted my joy of riding and certain things started to materialize as I imagined them. With this influx of change I resigned from my job and, to put it more bluntly, began to think deeply. I've come to the decision that the job I want to carry out is in the bicycle sector. This will revive me and deliver an immense will to work.

I wanted to contact you as the owner of the best store, a store which I often visited and thus made friends through. I offer you a pair of hands. I am actually writing to you taking a leap of faith; I really would like to work with you. Perhaps you'd like to try me first as a part-time employee either in trading or sales departments? I genuinely want to work at a reliable company within a market I put my heart and soul in. If you should ask me why Aktif Pedal after all; you happen to provide an organization I greatly admire in terms of its audience and work philosophy. There were moments when I personally attended to your customers at the shop during my visits. I can keep talking about bikes for hours.

I am attaching my résumé with this note. I will be extremely pleased if you respond should there be a need in your organization. I hope you give me the opportunity to present myself and my ideas to you in more detail.

Respectfully,

Gökhan Kutluer

My email message bounced back from seven of the addresses stating they were not valid. At least it meant one of them was correct. Only one was delivered to the recipient. I was over the moon after I received a positive response. Me and the shop owner set a date and time to meet. I felt great enjoyment of becoming a staff member of the shop I was once a guest of.

***

This company became my home. It provided me with wonderful memories. Also it gave me the chance to network in the field. As soon as my office hours finished, I used to descend to the shop. I listened to the unnerving questions of customers besides the shining bikes and the rubber smell. Back then, the idea of reinstating a blog popped into my head. I called my blog Denge Tekeri in which I presented information, useful data on bikes. The content was based on the chats I had back at the shop. Sometimes, this information made way for the customers to purchase bikes. In addition, I could tell people about bikes who wanted to ride a bike from scratch.

I quite benefited from my little blog. I made useful connections, plus I gained recognition. It was good for my position in the market. My relentless struggle against authority, my outbursts against injustices cost me short-lived experiences at workplaces. I ended up working in various brands. Fierce fights with my parents who demonstrated little trust in me became daily burdens after my resignation. I spent my days idling around, though our dynamic with my parents emotionally drained me. I decided to ride along the south coast of Turkey in order to keep distance from my parents and clear my head. With the help of my friend Seçil, one of the few like-minded people in the cycling business, I borrowed a tour bike from their shop.

On my fourth day of the tour I had a phone call. Tufan, a guy I followed on social media called me for a project for a bicycle magazine. I didn't know him in person. As I was overwhelmed by weariness because of the rain and storm in the Dardanelles, I returned to Istanbul and found out about the project in detail. Luck has it that within a few days, I met the people behind the project and was appointed as the editor of the magazine.

I had never actively been involved in anything related to bikes. Only one; the unique competition experience I gained as the Belkin team leader upon dear Ömer Yavru's assurance at The Presidential Cycling Tour of Turkey. Yes, I was writing. My blog was getting a lot of hits but, at the end of the day, the source of my income was different. Now, I faced a whole new world. I felt I was doing business on the right side of the fence.

***

I built strong friendships, made new connections and interacted with a whole new crowd. Unfortunately, after a few months of success, I was faced with the fact that progression was an illusion. Certain facts about Turkey, its cultural codes restrained me. I was criticised for being an elitist. "I did not address the public in a humble manner," according to my editor's note column in one of the issues against my piece written on James Joyce. We parted ways after a full year's tenure as my bosses and I had a conflict of opinion.

I wanted to get a grip on how cycling should digitally be recognized. Unfortunately, I decided to cancel my project. I had the urge to leave Turkey. I consumed my tolerance towards those in my field reluctant to pursue new ideas.

***

There were terrorist attacks, guns firing at night in a row, in my neighborhood. One day, as I was standing by my ex in a tube, or in the metro as in Turkish, a guy held a knife against me accusing us of being too intimate in public space. No one reacted. That exasperated me enough to justify my means to leave Turkey. Or should I call it the new Turkey, which has been created by Erdoğan?

Although, these were all instrumental in my determination which proved I had to hurry.

It was time to pack.

FREUD'S CHAIR

The realtor in Istanbul presumed that I wouldn't last a year in the flat I had just signed the release of. He was right, I was already drafting my to-do list for my departure six months from that day.

First, I had to handle the visa issue. I wanted to get one valid for a year. If I held a tourist visa, with my Turkish passport, the maximum duration I could stay in any European country was 90 days applicable up to 180 days from the day of entry. This meant I would get to stay three months in one country, however, I would have to leave for the next three months. When I would get a visa for one year, I was permitted to stay another 90 days within that three-month period, which was two attempts for me.

What I wanted was, in my pursuit of a brand-new life, everything related to my needs to be new, as well. For this purpose only, I purchased a new "lucky" printer in white and pistachio green. Plus, I bought three blocks of paper so I could print the necessary visa documents.

***

A firm provided me with a letter. I had helped out with their website, so my statement was that I freelanced for them. I attached it to a bank statement, highlighted the pay days just like a friend of mine instructed. She worked at the visa center outsourced by the embassies in Turkey. According to her statement the most important data in each document should specifically be highlighted. It was apparently a minor but effective detail when it came to the application process. The date and info of the flight booked should also be highlighted on the document in the same way.

In conclusion, I collected all documentation including my letter of request which stated my interest in doing research on cycling and its cultural implications in other countries. I stated that it was for a new book. Therefore, I required a long-term visa. I went to the consulate with that.

The initial time I had visited the consulate is still a vivid memory. I did some research prior to my visit in online forums to inquire about their general attitude, to understand their demands and to see the duration of the wait. This information pulled me down a notch. However, considering all my documents were intact, I didn't stress out so much.

The lady behind the desk was keen on chatting while she was going through my papers. I took the liberty to ask her whether she had read any comments about the feedback they got in online forums. Apparently, she didn't care about negative feedback. She claimed that the attitude they held towards people with insufficient documentation and those like myself who submitted satisfactory information was different.

While I was reminiscing about my past, I walked to the desk in my turn, passed the papers through the slot in a kind manner. As I had never violated my visa terms before there was not proper chat except for a few simple questions. Praying that I would get a visa valid for a year I left the building and made my way home to contemplate the second item in my to do list.

***

I played with my cats Siena and Niccolò. They seemed to have missed me a lot. I returned home, laid down on my grey Freud's couch with its one side facing the wall. My bike stood on the other side.

This couch was a hand-me-down from my pal Burak. Just like he did, it was where I had kept staring at the ceiling more often than not and made my most critical decisions. During my last days in Istanbul, Burak, whose emotional state was in ruins just like mine, constantly tried to persuade me leaving Turkey was the best decision. However, it was going to be me leaving him behind. The couch's filth was ironic. Not a day went by without wine or food staining it…

Sometimes we would rush to cook in order to clear our minds. We would eloquently clean the products, chop and cook seriously. It filled up our plates as well as our stomachs. Our smiles would last a little longer than a butterfly's lifespan, shorter than what it took for the meal to cool down. Notwithstanding, we would feel the joy within our deepest veins in that short instant.

***

My parents came to visit me once in a while. They would even stay overnight. I told them it wasn't necessary anymore; I was leaving Turkey… I called the realtor and upon his approval I went to see the second-hand shop owner from whom I initially bought my cooker. I wanted to let him know which furniture and appliances he could purchase from my flat. It is ironic how short I stayed in that flat. As we agreed there was only packing up left for me to do. Or losing it.. Whatever you call it…

My books, souvenirs I collected from the cities I traveled, stuffed toys, bike paraphernalia, clothes and shoes…There were lots to pack. I was going to leave my fake Christmas tree. Also, the small lights I used to hang around them which my cats so loved to knock down behind. I set out to separate each remaining item.

"This goes to the bin, so does this, I don't even remember why I bought this, that's broken, I don't use it anymore, I'll sell these bike parts to get rid of them, those are so old…" I rushed to get boxes when it proved necessary to send some stuff to my parents and ended up buying more boxes than I needed. I wanted to give away some of my new and almost-new gear so I asked my friend Burak if he knew anyone in his hometown who might need them. We met up the same night in my bedroom and I started throwing whichever outfit I handpicked at the door.

"This is brand-new! Why are you chucking it? This would have been good for you over there! Take at least this one with you! C'mon buddy, this suits you! Oh, hey look, I could use that one…" Burak was rambling while at the same time picking up the clothes I threw off the floor. I, on the other hand, was reluctant to do anything. I had never made sense out of all these ineffective things in my wardrobe for years. It was as if I were unburdening my load by each throw. With each piece of cloth, I was cutting a memory in half so that they don't live with me anymore…

***

It was time to cancel my current contracts when eventually all packing was finished. I canceled the internet, tv, water and electricity in order of importance. I bought my plane ticket. I was already counting the days for my departure.

I had set the date of my departure as April 30, Nihan's passing anniversary. It was the day that changed my whole life, and I wanted to put it right again. This way, I will have created a concurrent breaking point and set the records straight once and for all.

***

Two weeks before my permanent departure, I set out for Italy for a five-day visit when I received my one-year valid visa. The aim was to get to know the city. I was going to move to a place to stay, but first, I needed to become idle. After a couple of days in Milan and Lake Como, I hit the road to visit Bergamo and started looking for rentals on my laptop at the hotel's lobby. I listed the available lodgings by ascending order and sent all of them the same message. My message indicated that I had come to Italy to finish my book and that I'd need a place to rent short-term; I also attached my Instagram account for their interest. It didn't take long to get a response; a flat with two people was looking for a third tenant, so I was there to see the flat the next morning.

The house was in a town called Dalmine, eight kilometers from Bergamo. It had a nice garden. It was a two-storey villa in which the owner lived with her three kids on the ground floor. The flat on the second floor was up for grabs. It, too, had double floors. The top floor had three single rooms, a bathroom and a storage area with a few bits and pieces and an old single bed. The floor in the middle, our entry floor, had a kitchen and a lounge area with a small bathroom.

My room was eight square meters with a single bed, a simple desk and a built-in closet. That was all. It was such a tiny room that it was impossible to open the door and the closet at the same time. I had to close one to open the other. There were no windows, only a skylight; I had to use a wooden stick to open or shut it.

The owner had two sons and a daughter and said the boys were quite keen on football. I could play with them in the garden if I wanted to.

I left there saying I would move in on April 30th and went back to Istanbul.

I met a few friends during my stay in Istanbul.

"I want to give it a go. If I fail and come back, I will say, 'at least I tried'. This way I won't have to live with a big 'what if' all my life. But, for now I want to give it a go. I want to see how far I can go, assess what I can achieve by myself."

We sat in Caddebostan, one of my favourite neighborhoods in the Asian Coast of Istanbul. Overlooking the sea and chatting, my friends declared their support and respect for my decision to leave.

Last week in Istanbul, I let my parents know the day of my departure. I asked them to send a shipment truck to carry my stuff. The last item in my to-do list was done. Siena was going to stay with my parents, while Niccolò with Gökçe. As for me, I headed to the airport with 2 bags and two bikes.

TARGET LOCKED

I possess a particular temper, certain habits and way of thinking that my mother complains about. She always hoped, even asked me to fix myself since I was a kid. If only that hadn't caused another childhood trauma to form. Whenever my mother was faced with my temper, she relentlessly reminded me, "See, you're doing it again! Don't son, you get upset about it later." I shrug it off. We had a fight if she kept her judgmental tone. I always persisted to be my own person.

I never gave up on my strong-mindedness. Whether it is the correct attitude or not; the satisfaction of finding things out myself and the perpetual wisdom I gained through other means was irreplaceable. If I were asked to make a list of my characteristics, I would place my self-assurance and my tendency to cling on things I felt strong about at the top of this list.

"Yes, mom, I hear you. You've always felt irritated about the things I obsess over. You're still fussing over it. However, I am who I am."

***

If you really want something you have to obsess over it. At least, that is my attitude. The degree of obsession, what it makes you do, what it brings to your life, what it takes from you and many other things all depend on you. If you want to achieve a certain thing you must visualize it all the time, reflect on it and let go of the people or actions around you that could morph into obstacles in your path.

It won't be a problem if you take a breather. Besides, this way you might come across an opportunity you may have missed. However, if you're undoubtedly aware of what you desire and set your mind to it, you never lose focus and be on guard only to mingle with those who could support you. If you're not comfortable with the term obsession then you could paraphrase it as target locked.

My goal was to move to Italy and work there.

***

Italy has been a favorite country of mine since I was a kid. I adored its cuisine. Italy was the first country I looked up on the map. My first trip abroad was again to Italy. I would support Italy in football games. I would manage Italian teams in Football Manager, a virtual game. Once, Burak and I each picked Italian teams and started a new game. We had declared our own rules and decided to sell our players only inland. Our aim was, even in that virtual world, to increase the standard of good quality players and improve Italian football.

Whenever there was a discussion involving Renaissance in İlkay Sunar's lessons, they would immediately bring to mind my days in Italy. I would swim in my fantasies. Florence was a city I was already in love with, without having seen it. There are no words of my sentiments on my first visit. I had mere reasons to love Italy.

I was drawn to Italian brands. As a result, I had picked an Italian made carbon bike to symbolize one of the first turning points in my migrant experience.

My aims regarding migrating to Italy increased. It was precisely during November 2015 when I initiated actions towards achieving the life I dreamt of.

After I left my job and broke up with my girlfriend, my emotional state evolved towards instability. I was sitting in the realtor's office amidst the pensive moments of how I should respond to the question, "Will you sign a one or two-year lease?" The realtor, upon the dazzled expression on my face, drafted the lease for one year, essentially believing I could only last six months there.

That flat acted as a launch pad.

***

Thus, I had my ends at focus. I had to prioritize my objectives, it was imminent. As I mentioned in the previous chapter, there was a project I had been carrying out but was reluctant to maintain. I also had my independent work aside. That wasn't binding at all. I could make use of the company I worked at for obtaining a visa. My freelance work brought no employment benefits but that wouldn't cause a problem since the main thing in tourist visas was regular account activities.

This immediately had to follow an action plan. I checked around via my connections. It didn't take long for me to discover things in Italy were conducted more or less in the same grid as in Turkey. I found out I had to personally be there to get things done rather than email or Skype chats. This whole situation did not complicate the plan but rather accelerated the process.

In a way, I gladly welcomed the pick of my relocation city earlier than I had presumed. It was quite off-putting at the time. Now was the time to use the color cartridge of the printer. I found a map of Italy with the highest resolution and printed it out. There were many details embroidered on it; including regions, towns, distance from non-Schengen countries and more. My desire was to choose a spot on the map. It was my wish to reside in a new city for a while where I got to pick. Relocating to Italy from Turkey was itself an issue, I didn't want to end up having made a poor decision and then move again consequently.

I quickly had to find a job so I could claim a legal immigrant status. I did some research about the Blue Card which was good to hold both as a residence and work permit within the European Union. When I found out it was made available to those with a graduate degree and speakers with a high level of English in order to encourage the flow of qualified immigrants, I knew my target was clearer: to persuade the company I worked for to ensure that they couldn't employ an Italian to carry out a good enough job as I did then.

I was resigned to the idea that I had to stick to my own initiative. If I were to start a job through employment agencies as any other immigrant, I would be doomed to provide a lot of paperwork and it would be highly competitive. I had to find a job that would choose me over a local. Subsequently, I was to locate a company where I could conduct my profession in Italy. Bike industry that I started back in Turkey. I typed cycling and digital marketing on the search engine for jobs, looked up all the websites of Italian bikes, cycling gear, cycling accessory companies I could think of. I pinned them one by one on the map. Siena and Niccolò glared at me at both end of my desk at that moment.

I decided on Northern Italy.

Companies around Milan and Bergamo specifically made up more than half the cycling sector and one of these would be my next employment. But first, I had to make a decision. Which one would it be? Milan or Bergamo?

Rome, Bologna, Florence, Siena - the noor of my eye - even the southern provinces, they all crossed my mind. All in all, I was well aware when I boarded this ship that I had to act well-scheduled and rational. I didn't have much savings, which meant I shouldn't make a mistake. My final decision would be based on certain means such as rent prices, the quality of life, population, transportation, cycling facilities etc.

I was not brave enough to move from a draining metropol like Istanbul to another one. Moreover, I was in an escalating frenzy toward nature. I wanted to see alternative views around myself other than mere buildings. As I navigated my pen on the map within the direction of lakes, parks, mountains and peaks, and with less densely populated areas to top it all, I came across one place: Bergamo.

***

I discovered that your inner or spiritual focus should simultaneously harmonize with your provisional new life. You have to constantly think of your plan. There's got to be a yearning for it inside of you. Everything has to evoke "that" in you. Your desire and will power to attain your aimed life have to be in line with the plans you made. Most of all, you should only share these plans with the ones you love or with those whom you're sure care for your wellbeing no matter what.

Although I was not much of a believer, I tended to light a myriad of candles in churches in Turkey or whenever, wherever I traveled abroad. I wanted my wish to move to Italy come true. I also counted on the shooting stars on many starry nights… There were moments when I felt at a total loss. Days when I didn't make any progress… I even visited a bunch of renowned fortune tellers in those days. Be it coffee or tarot readings, they eventually tell you what you want to hear. Well, what I needed was to hear them say it anyway and to nourish my mind in the hope of more hope, so I always left their place with a smile on my face. I didn't lack any of the qualities of the kings who consulted their soothsayers just before they went on to war, did I? This was my battle… Chasing my own dream.

***

You should be prepared for any negative reactions from friends. Don't lose contact with the ones who support you or help you through this arduous journey. Believe me, those are your true brothers. On the other hand, you have to eke out the ones who constantly approach you with a script doomed for failure. The ones who make fun of you or act nonchalantly because they can't deal with their own misery. People who stand by you at the start of your journey will be the ones to count on. It's alright when your true friends reveal the other side of the coin, come upfront with a list of provisional challenges to warn you. The major problem would arise if they approach you with arrogance.

If you have a plan, an aim; you might have to unload some of your burden, past resentments that slow you down. This resembles a missile separating from its components after its launch. In all its likelihood, this weight might apply to individuals. Past heartbreaks. Unfinished conversations. When the time comes, if you manage to eliminate all this burden; it becomes easier to acquire determination. Rest assured, you'll be substituting some other alternatives in their stead.

FINAL HOURS

On April 30, 2016, I was at Atatürk Airport (the airport is functioning no more due to the "biggest Airport in the world" situated on the other end of the city), situated in European side of Istanbul, four hours before take-off to Bergamo. I was at the top form. I intended to get everything done in case of any possible last-minute misfortune.

I was so hungry that I dragged my luggage and my bike to the eating area and ordered Turkish bagel with feta cheese and orange juice knowing they cost far too much in an airport. I gulped them all down and called my father to let him know I made it to the airport before the check-in time.

Almost half an hour had passed. I visited the gents quite a few times already. My solar plexus always suffered for my jitters. I was well aware I had to divert my attention elsewhere. I needed to calm myself. Face, or more likely repress, my anxiety. I decided to read the book which ended up as me looking at the book's pages with an empty regard.

***

A scene from the movie Fight Club came to my vision. Edward Norton tried not to focus on the pain when there was a chemical spill on his hand. In vain he struggled to divert his mind to other focal points but he failed each time. A punch to his face brought him back to life and he embraced his pain. Just like Tyler Durden had stated, this was the most outstanding memory in his life and that he should not have missed it.

"Without pain, without sacrifice we would have nothing."

I had managed to survive the first hour and calmed down. Now I was able breathe properly, clenched less and had no pressing need to visit the toilet. My worries had diminished. I knew where I was headed. I had a place to stay in Italy and knew my flat mates. I shouldn't have panicked.

***

I approached the check-in desk to ask them how I should proceed to have my bikes on board with me. Bikes go under a special baggage category, in which you pay loads. I didn't have to wait for the regular check-in counter to open. I paid the fee and wandered off. From that moment on, I felt completely on my own. It almost felt like dying: my whole life flashed before my eyes. I was about to take action towards the life I have yearned for. Something everyone doubtlessly would do were they in my shoes. Yet, I couldn't hold back from questioning the state I was in.

"Should I have stayed and fought?"

***

I presented the character traits of a Gemini as in indecisiveness and poor time management. Reflexively, I gaze through the menus for a long time when in restaurants. It takes me a while to make up my mind and order. When it comes to ordering coffee, from the minute I queue at a café 'till I'm about to order I always hesitate in my choices of coffees. In the end, I end up with a coffee that I am not happy about almost always.

I had found myself in a similar situation, the only difference was, I was not pressed for time. I was able to take my time to think as long as I wanted to and not board that flight. I could make a U-turn right there and then and continue my life as before, chase alternative way-outs. That way, I could see the people I loved as often as I liked. Or, I embark on a new journey in solitude. Not to stay on the land I was born in. With the people I knew by heart.

Like babies running around in circles who have just learned to walk, I had two words on my mind which would slow down, and even, put a stop to this turmoil: mystery and curiosity. I was curious about the places I was planning to visit and I also wanted to decode the secrets that other cultures possessed. From where I stood, I was Gökhan Kutluer, nonetheless I wanted to see what I was capable of in the land where nobody knew me. Therefore, I got up off the grey seat in the waiting lounge and got in line.

When it came my turn I knew what I'd choose didn't matter. Italy's coffee was sublime either way.

***

Without looking back, since there was no one to wave goodbye to, after check-in, passport and security control, I arrived at the "passengers only" section. Going through all sorts of aromas; some spicy, some sweet, Turkish delights wrapped in colored foils and bottles of alcohol on display. I walked to my gate. It felt immensely relieving.

I sat down in the first available seat, took out my phone and typed a few email messages to the people who honored me in the quest of my dreams. I didn't know why I sent those messages. I had thanked the people a thousand times up until then and expressed my appreciation for their help. Perhaps, I genuinely believed this was a success story and that I wanted to show them their help had been a crucial stone in paving the path for me.

I also thought of informing some of my ex-girlfriends. I gave up the idea soon after. Honestly, I feared their responses. I feared receiving no response even more. On top of that, it wasn't that much necessary to show my generation was highly affected by Teoman, a Turkish pop-rock singer who wrote about pain, lust, loss and "love." Though, most of his love songs ended up being about miserable losses or confused make-up sexes. I was listening to his heart wrenching song Paramparça about being young, losing the father and having a fragmented soul. I had already been declared "that problematic guy" by all my exes due to my "unresolved" issues and/or instability.

Unlike the couple before me, I had held my passport and boarding pass ready. It was a matter of seconds to go through the last checks and get on the airport shuttle to take me to my flight. The shuttle bus looked compressed but spaced out inside. It was a regular pastime for my fellow people to ride in a chock full of vehicles and this was no surprise. Their usual hasty and aggressive attitude had upset me. Reminding myself this would be my last test to endure, I had managed to ride the shuttle without protesting and screaming.

It wasn't long before I was brooding over a train of thought in spite of the carrier's engine. As I was approaching the flight of stairs to the plane I felt like a kitten held by the scruff by his mother. Life had gotten its teeth into my scruff for my own safety and now was taking me to a mysterious journey so as to hide me in such nooks that even the most misbehaved kids could not find. The only difference was that I had none of my siblings with me.

Engrossed in what to do in times of trouble on my own, I boarded the plane ignoring the fake smiles of the cabin crew.

"Excuse me, that's my seat... D is not a window seat, F is…"

My seat belt was fastened, my sunshield was up and I didn't care if any signs were turned on.

FIRST SIEGE OF BERGAMO

This guy packs up and leaves
Worn out
Slowly departs from here
Bruised and dismal
This guy packs up and leaves

I remember listening to two of the tracks a lot more than others when the plane took off. One is *Gitti Gider* by Demir Demirbakan with the lyrics above. The latter, *Hareket Vakti (Time to Move)* by Umay Umay. The lyrics goes as "There's always something calling me from other cities far far away." I couldn't have enough of her heartbreaking voice. Although I wasn't someone with a refined or sharp music taste, I kept listening to these two tracks and their alternatives constantly on my iPod mini. Tracks after tracks of downers, and rebellion... That was my healing method when I suffered. To glorify it instead of soothing it, to let it sting instead of alleviating the pain... Typically I liked experiencing every sensation and emotion to the highest point because it felt impossible otherwise to manage these sensations without knowing everything about them. Bliss, melancholy, longing.. I was well aware I had to experience all these to the bone, that these were the nourishment of my soul. Now though, the challenge was to learn, absorb, and finally, to end the pain of parting.

***

Just before the plane started to descend, I finished taking notes. I removed my headphones and looked out of the window. Excited to see Bergamo ahead of me, a very warm feeling came over me. I was in a hurry to get off the plane. My landlord's oldest kid, Martina, was going to meet me at the airport. These were things on my to-do list. I didn't manage well in repressing my anxiety.

I didn't come across a problem at the passport control. An Italian officer glimpsed at me. He did not ask any questions or wanted to see my tentative return ticket. I passed through customs with ease and hurried to the baggage claim. My plan was to pick my bags first and then go collect my boxes. When I spotted my bike boxes arriving on the carousel as well. I figured my initial guess had been correct. Here, everything was compact, simple and modest.

I brought all my stuff together first and then checked if my bikes were in good shape. They were. I had to carry them all at once, so, congratulating myself on bringing some change with me I went to grab a trolley. I freed one inserting a two-euro coin and releasing it from its dock and walked toward the exit. Unfortunately, it was inevitable not to bump into people when pushing the trolley. I had placed the boxes horizontally, so the trolley looked three times wider than it was supposed to. Finally, I spotted Martina.

I had an overly exaggerated smile on my face while walking with Martina to her car. It felt silly. She had light brown tresses and a wonderful smile. Martina was tall, well-proportioned and friendly. I was extremely happy that everything went well and that we were on our way home at long last. We did small talk while walking to the car park. That kind of eased my anxiety.

Two rounds needed to be made to the airport since not all my boxes fit in the car. Martina left with some of my stuff. I stayed in the airport car park and waited for her next to my stuff. In the meantime, I sent some photos to my parents and to my friends to let them know, I survived the journey. I realised that I had purchased a mobile phone with a 16GB memory. It wasn't going to be possible to save a lot of pictures, so I deleted a lot. Mostly photos from Turkey that had a homely or warm feeling. I had to cut off the future possibilities for longing. New moments now had space to enter my 16GB phone. New landscapes, new songs, new acquaintances…

***

I averted my gaze from the screen when I heard a weak horn. Martina was driving me to my new home. Dalmine, a few kilometers from Bergamo, was famous for its garden houses and its university campus. The sun was out in the city center; but, I could see the rain clouds gathering in the distance.

Although I had seen it before I was excited as it was my first time in my new abode. Despite my momentarily extending excitement, I was unsure as to how long I would stay in Dalmine. Its door, windows, garden, mail box..

everything about it looked different. I was flushed, my face was burning up with joy. Only when my cheeks started hurting did I realize I had been smiling all along. After I greeted the landlord and his family, I carried my bags to my room and bike boxes to the garage. I didn't want to delay building my bikes. I wanted them ready so I'd be able to ride them.

Andrea, the middle child, came right up next to me asking too many questions. I guess, just like his older sister, he wanted to practise his English with me.

There was heavy rain. I took the stairs in twos and went straight into my bedroom. I took out the whatnots that I had placed on top of the pile in my bags and put them away. I then closed my door in order to lay on the bed stretched out in peace. My head resting on my arms... The raindrops I kept watching on the skylight reminded me of Virginia Woolf's description of "A Haunted House":

"The rain slides silver down the glass."

"Safe, safe, safe," the pulse of the house beat gladly.

It was quiet now. Apart from the occasional sound of the windswept trees I could hear nothing. The smell of earth that filled the living room through the curtains reached me. A sense of stillness came over me, my mind slowed down, my eyelids were heavy.

This was how I drifted into sleep on the first day of my new life.

I opened my eyes when one of my flatmates entered my room. He was making his rounds downstairs, it was dark. I got up, washed my face and went down to the kitchen. Gaspare was the one who had woken me up. He greeted me with a shamed expression on his face and apologized.

We struggled while communicating in English. I tried talking to him in my A1/A2 Level Italian. It wasn't as bad as first timers.

I found out Gaspare who was swarthy, green-eyed, a little shorter than I and a bit chubby, was originally from Sicily. I had heard people from southern Italy were usually warm-hearted. Gaspare turned out to be just like I imagined him. He was genuine and calm. He confessed that he had put on weight after a knee operation as he didn't do any sports. I realized I wasn't going to have any problems with him.

Gaspare also told me our other flatmate Alberto was married. Apparently, Alberto worked hard. He would go to see his wife and kid in Padova on the weekends. While updating me on all this he prepared dinner for both himself and me. I noticed how big his portion was while he was cooking for himself. At some point, I realised he was cooking for us both.

Time flew by as our conversation carried on covering Turkey, Italy, football, girls, food and my bikes which I parked there as soon as I arrived. Time was flying by. I was enjoying the things that I liked. What was strange was how long I stayed at the dinner table. Since my time in Siena, I was acquainted with the fact that Italians took their dinners seriously. The ones I knew loved spending a great deal of time between the courses. I was capable of sitting at the table calmly for hours without displaying any sign of anxiety. On my to-do list, I had "eat pizza from across my home's street." However, the meal (not pizza) prepared and served by my new flatmate certainly uplifted me. It also eased the emotional and the physical fatigue that sunk from the travel.

***

I didn't feel drowsy at all; my afternoon nap together with the adrenalin pumped into my system by the bliss I felt had worked. To show my appreciation I did the dishes and cleaned up the kitchen. After watching some TV, I decided to take a shower hoping it would make me sleepy. I had a small orientation of the premise, checked out my reflection in the mirror. The color of the walls and the ceiling got reflected in the mirror. This was going to be my new visual reality.

***

"Am I really here?"

I unpacked Joyce's Dubliners from a box and continued reading from where I had left off. Joyce is a writer who voluntarily settled upon going into exile for a period. He experienced the shift between the urban and the rural. Evidently, it must have nourished his writing. Also, helped him thrive.

According to Joyce, his life was thoroughly transformed after he had moved to Dublin. In his own words "his life got dirty." In my irrelevant case, I had come to Bergamo from the hustle and bustle of Istanbul in order to write my first book. But I also wanted to "cleanse." Would my life change as much as Joyce's did, after he left Ireland? I wondered. Would I be able to finish writing my book like he did? Or, would I be able to continue writing after that? Would I have to move to another location for the new book then? I completely got distracted with these thoughts and stopped reading. Soon after I became sleepy. I passed out.

***

I woke up to the day on May 1st, 2016. Everywhere was dead silent. In part I was happy and dazed because I was used to waking up to my kitties' play noises, high-pitched talks of passersby on the street regardless of the time of day. Regardless of the noise of the emotional and physical sibling abuse coming from downstairs.

My plan for the day was to do some shopping, get to know Bergamo a bit and arrange my room. But first, I went around to where my bikes were and took them out. Actually, I was so eager that I grabbed both of them and brought them downstairs. Then I walked across the road and took a picture of them and the house in the same shot.

I was unable to catch up with the number of comments and likes my Facebook post received like no other. I was ready for people's reactions, curiosity and appreciation, but I truly had never expected this. It was as if everybody had been aware of my dreams and they couldn't wait for me to leave Turkey… Seeing what people, some friends, wrote and how happy they sounded because I had made it, proved that I had done the right thing.

I put my phone away, went up to my room, opened my bag and took out my computer to set it up. I had bought the computer from Onur, whom I had met through my cycling friends. Onur had the loveliest daughter and his wife was very gracious. When I purchased the computer and was having problems setting it up. Onur came and helped me although it was nearly midnight. He had a heart of gold as well because he knew of my financial and psychological struggles. He was easy on the payments.

By then I started taking out my clothes, my red and white checkered bedding and everything else that was related to bikes. After I was settled, I got out of my room to obtain a perspective to my new life from the outside: I gazed at the room I settled in. Everything was clean, tidy. As my new start. There was only one thing missing. When I went downstairs and brought one of my bikes back to my bedroom.

"Aha!" I said. Now it looked gorgeous.

***

Dalmine was overcast and a bit windy. Clearly it was going to rain. Therefore, I dropped the idea of going out on my bike. When I finished my work, I went one street up and started waiting at the bus stop for a ride to the city center. The schedule indicated the bus's arrival in two minutes. I distracted myself on my phone for quite a while, walked up and down the street. There was no bus.

I felt the anxiety grabbing me into its nasty palms so I asked one of the passersby the bus's arrival. He told me that on May Day the busses wouldn't run until after midday.

I felt pointless, stuck in Dalmine. The small town didn't have many means of transportation to the city center. First moment of "crisis" that made me realize I was no longer in Turkey. Workers, civil servants were allowed to have a day off on their special days. Presumably, they were also allowed to freely celebrate in the city.

"Of course! Let them have their days off. Screw it, I'll go later. I am here now for good!"

Instead of going back home, I went straight to what was called Dalmine's village center. There were elegant villas, a few cute shops, a couple of supermarkets on the way. After a roundabout, I was there. I spotted a street sign showing where the ice cream shop, the café, the pharmacy, the post office, university campus and a Tabacchi were. There it was, all closed, yet I had found it.

I left there feeling quite discontented. Puppies would do anything for a bite of their owner's food but have to stick to their pet food in their bowls.

This analogy captured my mind when I realized I had to turn around and leave.

***

The first few days in Dalmine were going well. Nevertheless, there was non-stop rain. Plus, my battle against the mosquitos that were taking advantage of the non-disinfestation philosophy of the city in order to protect a few bug species, was a big one. I spent my days playing football with my landlord's kids, reading, writing my book, listening to music and, best of all, going food shopping with Gaspare and then coming back home and cooking.

I said 'best of all' because I love living with people I get on well with under the same roof and doing things together with them. It was probably because I'd never had a chance to experience anything similar to this with my elder sister Nihan that I missed simple things like these. Many emotions shared between two siblings were always absent in my life. During my high school years, I loved it when my friends came over to stay with us. We would play computer games and have breakfast the next morning. I even slept in the guest room with my friends to chat before we went to bed sometimes as we had two single beds in that room. My mom liked most of my friends. She would take care of them just like she took care of me. Therefore, what I precisely used to feel then was playing house. It felt great for my soul to live even for a day with a fraternal brother.

***

The residual effects and feelings of starting a job as soon as I had finished university were still raw. A young and inexperienced person, unsure of his aspirations about life, to plummet into professional life resulted in consecutive days of despair. I did not want to relive it. Therefore, I tried to take things easy this time; although, my current situation was already challenging. I tried to get used to my new surroundings first. Only after I got used to the weather, to the habitat, to the people and to the culture did I feel free to look for work.

"It's by riding a bicycle that you learn the contours of a country best, since you have to sweat up the hills and coast down them. Thus, you remember them as they actually are, while in a motor car only a hill impresses you, and you have no such accurate remembrance of the country you have driven through as you gain by riding a bicycle." Reflecting on Ernest Hemingway's quote, I felt whole-heartedly ready to discover Bergamo.

Located on hills like the Acropoli, Bergamo was a city divided into two. There was a historical upper district and a modern, urbanized town below. Città Alta, a UNESCO world heritage, built within the walls by the Venetians, reflected what all other Italian cities possessed. Its cobblestone streets, gigantic city gates, low-rise buildings and their cute shutters took people centuries back. Città Bassa, lower city, was built due to population growth. With its avenues it expanded to become a rather larger territory.

But, this was not all.

Bergamo caught my heart by its nature. The city, its Alpine lakes and hills made my mouth water. I had got myself located right in the heart of a geography where Giro d'Italia took place, a race I had watched for years on TV. And I wanted to get on my bike and ride to discover all those woods, mountains and hills.

And so I did.

I checked the Strava website and found most ranked routes and climbs around the area. I also found the locations with bike shops. There were brands and a wider product range that were non-existent in Turkey. I purchased a few items that I needed either from their main shop or at their outlet shops.

During one of my rides I met up with Marco who lived in Bergamo. He worked for a brand that represented a distributor with whom I worked back in Turkey. He was around the same age as me. Marco was well-educated and happy to be working in the bicycle industry. We were in close contact before I left Turkey. He told a lot about the city, its geography from him. I was ready to go on long rides by myself now.

So I got on my bike.

To the north one day, south the next... One day I headed to the west and another, east... I rode until tears fell from my eyes and my legs abandoned me because of fatigue. I rode until I was snowed up in San Marco Pass, until

I swore with pain in the last kilometers in Valcava. My bike's saddle had become the epitome of an ideal place to provide my mind with the clarity it coveted. Sometimes just to flee from problems or rather, solve them... I would transform into a completely different person when I pedaled. I challenged myself, had talks with old friends I'd had issues with or thought about my ex. A type of introspection; perhaps it was some sort of therapy.

The track that constantly played in my mind was *Başka Türlü Bir Şey (Something Different)* by Yeni Türkü. Each time I listened to this song, I was overwhelmed by emotions.

"A delightful journey descends into the ground from a branch, ever high as the tree, ever high as the branch, in the wind... And it's a whole new life in the grass you arrive at, in all its green…"

Tears fell onto my cheeks while pedaling. They poured down on the handlebar. I still rode; falling into reverie on those mountain tops I had climbed one by one. The World looked so awesome from high up… Everything related to people stayed afar and small. Not a soul was able to touch me.. at least for a while.

Naturally, peace never lasts forever, I would get cold at long intervals despite my stored body fat. Keeping my promise to myself, I watched every bite I ate as I had put on weight in Istanbul. Tough climbs were somehow my payback. I modified all my food shopping, my meal times and portions. I didn't have to lose five kilos per month or there were no lower limits. I only wanted to eat well; to benefit more from organic products that nature presented while I so enjoyed nature because it was good both for my body and soul.

***

As the end of May approached, the scents of everything new started to disappear. The way I perceived the complications around me was down to normal; I had now discontinued eyeing everything around me in awe. I had realized I was at a crossroads. No longer a tourist or nor a resident in a place… I had visited every possible corner in Bergamo. There were no Lake Como or beautiful towns surrounding it, nor Lake Garda or Iseo left to see…Or Milan or Bergamo's towns, large or small… I had been to every neighborhood I could reach by bike without spending much money.

The water leaking on my bed when it rained hard, unstable internet connection, mosquitos finding their way in through half-open windows because there were no AC's or seeing the condo I had just cleaned or tidied up being back to its old appearance within a short while. All these had started getting on my nerves.

It was obvious that it was time I had to make a list of actions in order to stay here. Or else, I would be just like one of those retired army officials who picked up a fight against every object or person that came their way…

JOB HUNTING IN ITALY

There was a guy called Rene who I met back when I was working in the magazine. It was during one of the launch conferences. He was a partner at a leading equipment brand. Thanks to the questions I'd asked during the conference along with our dialogue following the event, I had a chance to sit with him. He happened to have a lot of questions regarding penetrating the Turkish market and, as the editor of the only cycling magazine in Turkey, I had to provide him with information. I briefed him over lunch about all things he wanted to know in light of my field experience, observations and outcome of my discussions with colleagues. I had managed to get Rene to grow an interest in the bike market in Turkey during lunch.

That lunch can be considered a token of a few memorable events that allowed me to be proud of myself. Not only had I impressed Rene and his colleagues from Italy, but I had also left a good mark on other guests in the same industry whose English needed improvement. I was ecstatic on the way back. I knew I had achieved something that could be good for me in the future, however, as I had not yet groomed the idea of immigrating from Turkey back then. No attempts were made in that direction yet.

***

The Monday following my third weekend in Bergamo, I opened my laptop and updated my resume. New address, phone number and a cover letter that could be sent to any company, any brand. There, I was ready!

I aimed at companies around Bergamo and Milan first. The email I sent was nothing to write home about. I had introduced myself briefly, and wanted to prove how determined I was, though just as I was convinced much later, there was never a good time to check those emails sent to "info" addresses.

I had tried to make it fun in order to shake off its dullness. I dedicated myself to one concept a day and I wrote an email to the brand representing that concept. One day I wrote to companies that had a four-letter name, another day, to the companies that contained no imprints in their names, another, to those that were based in southern regions in Italy… This way, I had managed to forward my resume to all the companies I'd had in mind.

This was the first thing I dealt with each morning. Then I'd jump on my bike. I pedaled along. While riding my bike I used to think I had already had a job at one of the companies. I would visualize how it would feel to be there, having imaginary conversations in my head. It was a grand feeling to dream while riding; it seemed there was nothing a well-nurtured mind couldn't achieve to think. I dreamed I worked at each company in various capacities. The idea made me happy. I presumed my office was close-by. Therefore, I would ride my bike one day. I'd walk to the office another day. On a rainy day, my colleague who lived further down the road would pick me up in his car. My salary wasn't that bad, either. There were no limits to the food I consumed and I could go on a long weekend trip every other month.

Unfortunately, those pink clouds that held thousands of dreams would disperse the minute I got off my bike. It left me with nothing; but a few memories of a road trip. Also, perhaps, a solitude that could be defined as calmness.

***

I grew up in a house full of negativity. The whirlwind of disharmony convinced me to believe I was an unfortunate being. I lived in guilt, shame and self-loathing for a long time.

Whenever I was on the brink of doing something I had taken up a routine of perpetually preparing myself for a worst case scenario to come. So, I forced myself to not get too excited about anything. It was exactly for this reason I had approached job hunting in Italy in the same way. Despite my pessimism, I had an awkward self-assurance. I kept my hopes up. Regardless of all the rejections I had received in a land where I couldn't speak the language very well. I believed in myself. Plus, there was nothing for me back home. It was a struggle to not anticipate the probability of going back. The only thing that worked was to fully focus on the present. I only planned the next step, not the foreseeable future. The future is in the future.

My initial attempts of finding a job didn't produce a substantial result. Thus, I decided to extend my search through close contacts. I went to the closest: my landlord. I asked if we could have coffee together. During our coffee, I briefed him about my desire to migrate to Italy. He found my wish courageous and left saying he would think of what he could do.

I also reached out to some of the people I knew well in the Turkish industry. Some directors, asking them if they could forward my resume to the companies or distributors they were in contact with. I didn't have such high hopes. Their demeanor was nice. I also knew deep down they might not lift a finger. At any rate, I was in Italy now. I distracted myself from the idea of asking for help since I didn't want to feel indebted to someone. I never contacted anyone in the industry for any matter ever again.

Just as I was getting down to sending a second round of emails to the companies I hadn't heard back from, a buddy of mine from Switzerland came to Italy with a startup idea on mind. Similarly, his arrival gave me the opportunity to polish up my resume. His magic touch on both the format and the content in my resume certainly got it in shape to be better noticed. This time, I sent it only to the brands that I would be happy to be a member of.

During a few days I took a break from job hunting. I went to Switzerland and finished my now in second edition storybook, *Cloud Factory*, in one of the villages between the Germany and Switzerland border. I was pretty pleased to have finished my book and also finished my search for the name of my book. So, I went back to Italy as a satisfied man.

***

Back in Istanbul during our working lunch with Rene, I had gathered that I was definitely in his good graces. Unfortunately, it was too late when I found out the brand he represented had been looking for a rep. It didn't take long for me to persuade him that it would be a good attempt to appoint someone who would introduce the recently launched bike wheels to the Turkish market. Thankfully, Rene did send them to me. However, the wheels had arrived weeks short of my departure from Turkey. Moreover, they didn't have their tyres on yet. Each time I searched for suitable tyres for those wheels I ended up checking the only Italian website selling the products. As I didn't have enough time I had ordered them immediately because I didn't want to leave Turkey without taking any photographs of them.

When I received the tyres several days later I photographed them together with the wheels and sent them to the general email of the website quoting my appreciation of their dispatch on the same day of my order. I went on to my first ride with them, took a few more photos and posted them on my social media after receiving a short but sweet response from Andrea. Both the wheels and the tyres were great but somehow there seemed to be a skip in the same spot. It was possible that the valve was misplaced. Or perhaps, I had made a mistake when I installed them as Gökçe and I were busy chatting nonstop during that operation. As I was running out of time, I thought, once in Italy, I would definitely find some people who could take care of that problem for me.

***

I was in quite a good mood in Bergamo. My landlord Valerio informed me about someone he knew who was able to connect me with a renowned cycling clothing company. I was over the moon. They offered me to participate in an event after the much-expected annual velodrome organization. To find an opportunity to introduce myself very shortly would be enough since I had the capacity to present myself at my best. The major issue was to introduce myself.

I didn't want to leave everything relying upon one alternative so I made up my mind to drop by the office which I had written the tyre skipping problem to. My aim was to talk briefly about myself and, in a natural flow of things, bring the topic to job opportunities in the bike industry in Italy. After a few emails we agreed to meet the same evening. It was so hot and humid that I was soaked by the time I got to Curno from Dalmine, which is only a few kilometers apart. When I reached the address I noticed there wasn't any sign of a store or a shop window so I called them. It was then I found out they didn't have any actual shops, they were only doing e-commerce.

I met Andrea, he had a warm smile. He was back from walking his dog. When we went in, I started looking round her office. Bikes, frames, wheels, desks here and there, books on dust-covered shelves and many other stuff scattered around… I was more intrigued about the company's different products other than customized steel bicycles. While he was changing the tyres Andrea and I kept on chatting. He was gathering information about me. In the meantime, I was thinking if I could picture myself working there in the future. I talked about what I did, and mentioned my skills during our conversation. After nailing that elevator pitch I got on my bike and rode back home. Andrea made it clear by his gestures that he wanted to be left to his own devices.

I have to iterate here how in awe I was that after all the ramifications in my life. Things turned out my way. It is true that every cloud has a silver lining. Wasn't it amazing that tyre problem which I couldn't solve back then found its way here, where I now belonged to?

***

Just as I was putting the weight I had lost back on due to rains storming through Bergamo that had me housebound, Rene invited me to his office. He had received my email which informed him of my presence in Italy and that I wanted to see him. My next step was to move forward with our connection.

On a shitty rainy Tuesday I got on a bus to go to his office. I had taken the wrong transfer bus. I got off the bus two kilometers away from his office. There was a lot of rain and I didn't have an umbrella with me. Tried my best to get away from the rain as much as possible... I tried to make my hair presentable before I buzzed him. It was exciting to be knocking on the door of an office I had checked on Google maps just a few months before.

I climbed the spiral staircase, my footsteps echoing on the dark wooden floor. I passed the dramatic colored walls and went into the conference room to wait for Rene. One of the books shelves, Campagnolo caught my eye. I picked it up and started scanning it. It was the story of how the brand started and grew. However, I was only able to look at the photos with my limited Italian. Soon, I heard Rene's voice. He was approaching the conference room while talking on the phone. He was engaged on the phone a few more minutes and then joined me. He seemed fine, inquired about my days in Italy and afterwards came to the point. He told me about how the company operated, what lacked and what was needed. I didn't have to explain myself as he obviously knew why I was there.

I told Rene about my job experience, what I did and what I wanted to do here. I touched base on discrepancies on internet sites along with social media accounts and summarized the paths to be followed to fix these. He listened to what I said attentively. Though, the expression on his face wasn't the face of an impressed man.

He finally blurted it all out. The company was in urgent need of a sales person. On the other hand, what I mostly talked about involved marketing. When I understood the supply and demand didn't match I became silent. Actually, there was no failure here. In other words, I didn't leave this first official interview defeated. Still, I sulked. Rene noticed this and said that he would send me a personality test via email as he valued its outcome. He saw me out and I started walking back to the bus stop, spent, my head bent and my feet turned inwards.

I was sure this process wouldn't end on a positive note. I wasn't going to give in. Enrico, who worked at Bianchi store in Bergamo, Andrea from Cicli Corsa, my most solid connection Rene, my landlord Valerio, and last, Elena from the HR department at the textile company… Apart from a few others which I didn't list here, I had had my most serious meetings with these people, and if anything at all should happen, it would be through one of these contacts.

I quickly cheered up and was ready the weekend after to meet the family at the organization at the velodrome. Hiding my bitten fingernails in my pockets, I think I did well though a little showed off. Things I knew about the bicycle itself and its trend was my strongest skill. The stuff I found about the family members through interviews and magazines, I had managed to secure a marketing job interview within a few days.

Meanwhile, some friends in Turkey were taken aback by my posts on social media and they were keen on joining me for a bike ride in Italy. One of them, whom I got to know just before my departure, was Emre. Young, vibrant, curious and energetic, Emre was a guy who had every confidence in himself that he could achieve anything he had put his mind to. A couple of phone calls after, dates were set and before we knew it we found ourselves by the hills and lakes surrounding Bergamo.

Those days we toured felt wonderful to me because I had appreciated once again that those memorable moments became more precious when shared with those who had total understanding of you. If there are any moments when I didn't feel lonely, apart from the times I played ball with my landlord's sons, Andrea and Giacomo, they most definitely are the times I shared with Emre. We had such a great time together that even the coinciding coup attempt in Turkey didn't destroy our fun. We had called our loved ones after watching the latest news through poor internet connection in my tiny bedroom. And once we were convinced they were alright, we were sound asleep, happy to be up and ready for the next day's bike route.

I WILL BE BACK

I got more stressed out as my 90-day stay was about to expire. I bit my nails harder and walked about the house on end. Even my grocery shopping was at a low as I didn't want to eat. Eating once or twice a day perhaps wasn't good for me but it sure was good on my budget. Bergamo's never-ending rainy days and the dark clouds depressed me even more; that tiny room I got myself locked-in had slowly become a dungeon I couldn't get out of. I was in a race against time, my eyes were dry and burning because I couldn't keep staring at the computer screen for a response.

I couldn't ride my bike, I couldn't focus on my book.

I needed a new plan.

***

Going back to Turkey was not an option. I didn't want to feel defeated, surrendered or unsuccessful. So, I was looking for a way out. I decided to make an assessment among the non-Schengen countries where I could spend a productive summer.

Albania was the first country that came to mind but after I scanned through the cities on the internet I opted out of it. The streets I walk should possess some sort of an attraction to me.

Wishing Croatia weren't an EU state, I went on to study Bosnia. By eliminating its cities one by one I came to the conclusion that some place with a long coastline would work for me.

Macedonia was too inland and Serbia didn't promise anything other than Belgrade.

What I got in the end was Montenegro.

***

I was running really low on budget. The easiest and least worrisome way to find accommodation and food was through finding a job there. My observations in Bergamo revealed that most restaurants were hiring summer interns who studied tourism and hotel management. This meant that tourism season was on. Checking out jobs at hotels and travels agencies would be a good option.

A fortnight into my visa's expiration, as each sip of the bitter coffee from the porcelain mug burned my lips I started my search.

Certain hotels were quite in the luxury category. Some seemed pretty corporate-like. I needed somewhere that contained more air of leisure in it. Somewhere warmer and that could carry me…I sent around a chain of emails and then went on to send some to the hostels. When on the same day I received a response from Hostel Montenegro which had branches in Podgorica, Budva and Kotor, I got on my bike and rode in a frenzy for kilometers. Not even the rain could ruin my excitement. I climbed, got soaked, felt chilly at the peak, nearly froze on the way down but never stopped dreaming or fictionalising my future there. Even envisioning certain things was so relaxing…

I described my job experience in the email I wrote. I also mentioned my level of English. I asked for nothing but a room and board. Receiving their genuinely sincere response in return made me anticipate what lay ahead of me with hope. Things would work out fine. I felt it.

***

Now, I needed to find a way to get to Montenegro, where I would soon notice the best Islamic call to prayer was recited. I didn't want to take suitcases with me. My reasoning was simple: it was a totem for me. Suitcases meant home.

"I'll leave my suitcase here, I will surely be back."

I told my landlord the situation and started getting my backpack ready. A few shabby t-shirts, two pairs of shorts, a toothbrush, some other stuff and, on top of those, my bike gear. I was ready to travel without disassembling or boxing my bike. I had shared my recent plans with my family and friends and they all thought my plans were hazardous. I didn't pay attention to their catastrophic scenarios. On the contrary, after all those talks, traveling to another country with my backpack proved to be a challenge from then on. I was neither sure of how long I'd stay there nor what I would face…

I dedicated myself to the notion that my transit from Italy to Montenegro was to be unforgettable and, at the same time, romantic. Therefore, I came to the conclusion that I would travel first by train and then by ferry. They were the two most romantic means in my opinion. I purchased my tickets for the next day and was ready to travel. I was going to go to Milan from Bergamo, then to Bari and then to Bar on a ferry. Afterwards, the only thing to do was to get on a train to Podgorica and reach the hostel.

This never happened.

***

There have been many moments in my life when I missed major details and put my life at risk.

Once, after we finished a bike tour with Burak in Copenhagen. We lost a lot of time and money because I misremembered our flight's departure and arrival times.

A similar incident happened in my mid-twenties when I was in Siena. I had missed the coach to Milan then. And after that, I missed the flight to Oslo… Well, it was a bad coincidence that on the same day David Beckham was in town after the announcement of his Milan transfer but still.. the traffic got screwed because of his arrival. However, it was my bad.

I get carried away within the notion of road tripping. My pupils turn into smiling emojis. They stop me from seeing the important details.

***

Spacey carriages, pleasant seats, a dimly lit aisle and a soft carpet… I couldn't find a spot to park my bike on the train from Milan to Bari.

Also, because I didn't pack my bike I wasn't able to leave it where the other travel boxes were collected. At the exact moment the officer approached me and asked me to get off the train. A chill ran down on my back. He couldn't express himself in English, nor I, in Italian…

I mentioned that I would be reimbursed for my ticket. First, I needed to digest getting out. I sat at a stinky café in Milan's train station and ate something chocolaty.

Once I collected myself I got in line downstairs in the ticketing office. So many people were looking at me. Waiting in a queue with my bike made me the center of attention. I waited there, my bag on my back and my bike next to me...

After a few phone calls, it was my turn. I told them about the situation and showed them my ticket. I was alone, stunned in anticipation. I was only accompanied by typing sounds of the keyboard and the green reflection of the computer on the woman's glasses. It took only a few seconds but felt like at least ten minutes. If I were only able to waste less time in the café, I found out, I would have received my reimbursement.

The conductor was trying to tell me something. It got lost in translation. I was supposed to claim reimbursement of my ticket within an hour of the train's departure...

I was going to pay and collect the ferry ticket when I reached the port. I immediately canceled my booking. The train ticket fee had hit me hard.

I proceeded on to the platform fatigued after purchasing a Bergamo ticket from one of the vending machines among their irritating automated warnings to be extra careful about theft. With my remaining lasting power, I managed to pick my bike up and place it in the wagon. Then I carried myself to the next seat vacant.

The moment Gaspare saw me at the gate that afternoon he was gobsmacked. He offered me food. I was unable to do anything else but drink gallons of water and then went back to my room.

I showered in freezing cold water after informing the hostel that my arrival date and time would be delayed. I lay on the bed looking up at the sky through the skylight.

I had to make plans again. This time, it was imminent...

***

Taking the same route crossed my mind. I could have opted for boxing the bike and travel first on the train and then the ferry, but I had lost my appetite. Also, the train ticket was up from the day I had purchased mine. I didn't check flights since, this time, I would be paying for the boxes on top of my air ticket. I was being pulled by the direction of going on the motorway. It was time to click the Bla Bla Car ads that kept appearing on my screen.

I had to use my mobile phone as my computer was disassembled and in my bag. I downloaded the app, subscribed to check whether there were any cars going from Bergamo or Milan to Montenegro. There was one heading to Slovenia. I could then continue to Montenegro, still I couldn't be sure if my bike would fit as it was a small vehicle. When I scrolled down, I found a bigger car going to Albania. It appeared one of its seats was already occupied but two seats were available. I looked up its route; it was going to Tirana driving on the shore. I sent a message right away.

He requested 15 Euros and didn't charge extra for my bike or my bag. So, I declared that I could pay for two seats. However, he said that wasn't necessary and as soon as I booked my seat he retrieved his plan from the offers list. I was lucky. I was going to ride on the back of the car by myself and didn't need to box my bike. I gave him my address in Bergamo and we agreed to meet at six in the evening the next day.

I wanted to take a good night's sleep to fully rest as I was never one of those people who could fall asleep on a ride. The next morning, I closed my backpack, had breakfast at my favorite place, watched some tv, had a pizza with a lot of toppings and went outside to wait for him an hour before we had agreed to meet. I left my bike, helmet and rucksack by the fence and sat on the sidewalk.

I like taking action before certain things happen. For example, if I know how much my total shopping will cost at a supermarket I queue up with the exact amount in hand. I don't like checking my pockets and looking for money. Nor making people wait… I used to get annoyed with my girlfriend who didn't take out her keys before she entered home. It used to drive me insane to wait for her while she searched for the house keys in her purse.

I heard an engine running and noticed a black SUV approach as I sat there resting my elbows on my knees and cupping my chin in my hands. I immediately got up on my feet. Two happy faces got out of the car. The guy sitting on the right had glasses on. He was pretty young. He spoke English with a German accent. The driver was a little chubby and paternal looking. We chatted briefly. When, after a couple of minutes, I tried to put my bike in the trunk. We had a little crisis going because the guy with the glasses, who turned out to be Lebanese German, was a musician and he had brought a few instruments with him. Though the trunk was huge, I still didn't want to risk any harm to my bike so I removed the wheels and placed the frame next to the instruments. I was going to take the wheels with me in the back as there was a vacant seat. The musician stated that he had concerns over his very expensive instruments. Thus, he asked me to take his instruments with me in the back seat and place both the wheels and the frame in the trunk.

We were ready to leave.

***

I was going on a thousand kilometers long road trip. Tears filled my eyes as we drove by. Bergamo faded away. I pulled myself together to keep my positive perspective intact. I emailed some people letting them know I left Bergamo. I switched off my phone and started chatting to the guys in the car.

It turned out our driver was Albanian and worked in Milan. Every few months he visited home to see his family and be with friends. I had noticed some gifts nicely wrapped in the trunk and understood he had kids but I didn't ask him how many. The Lebanese German musician in the passenger seat was touring the world with friends and busking. His bandmates stayed in Italy to join him later in Croatia.

A shared history, similar terminology, the same dishes but different names, comparisons between two nations' ladies.. all of these were the start of a nice chat with the Albanian driver. If I hadn't arranged a job in Montenegro I would definitely have gone to Tirana with him. That was how much I liked talking to him. He had been to Istanbul. Apparently, each of his trips was more on a grey-scale than the one before. I shared my most sincere sentiments with him about Istanbul as a city in the process of destruction, a process that is even perceived by the visitors. Then I put my head on the car window for a nap.

It was already dark when we went past Trieste road sign. Now we were on the opposite coast of the Adriatic and we'd had less than ten hours of drive left. Our first rest stop was in a town called Kozina. Coffee, stale bread, neglected toilets and a grim person at the till were all it took us to get back to the car and continue our drive before doing some flexing exercises.

The voices of the driver and the musician's sounded like whitenoise. Yet, I was still unable to doze off. We had two stopovers in Croatia. The first was the village of Ličko Lešće. Then, we stopped at Split. When we reached the cross borders between Bosnia Herzegovina and Croatia there was a long line. It was summer, July and the season was in full cycle. We waited as the situation necessitated. Each of us took turns to get out of the car and walk. The awful part of it was that the whole performance was yet to be repeated. We were passing Croatia and getting to Bosnia Herzegovina. In a few kilometers, we were supposed to enter Croatia again. Thankfully, we didn't encounter any problems on either side of the borders. Though the border officers did look at us weirdly, probably thinking, "What the heck would all these guys be doing? One Turk, one Albanian and one German." All in all, they were fine about everything and we were let pass.

Our last stopover was in Dubrovnik where we would drop the spectacled musician off. I so want to visit that city we passed by that day, soon. I haven't had a chance yet. There was supposedly a touch of Italian on Croatia's coastline. I wanted to visit Croatia for that reason. However, the timing wasn't right. The early morning hours had given us a break so we grabbed freshly cooked food to eat and right after, continued our journey. Montenegro was hours away. I honestly didn't care about how sleepy or tired I was. I was too excited.

Fresh air on my face, dark blue sea ahead, and hills above every way... I watched to the Bay of Kotor pass by. It greeted me with good wishes. I realized we were on the last minutes of our trip. I was dying to know what was ahead.

"What if I can't get on with the people at the hostel?"

"What if their rooms are stuffy?"

"I wonder if Podgorica is a very boring city?"

I warded off my questions of angst. I went to play Whack-A-Mall at a fairground. I hit the moles, sent them back into their holes immediately and enjoyed the scenery.

After we reached Tivat we continued driving on the coast toward Bar. The traffic jam made me think of Turkey. I realized that I was in a country with a small national economy. I kept on observing other properties of Balkan culture. It put a smile on my face.

Due to the traffic and the inconvenience caused by narrow roads, it took us two hours to get to our final point instead of one. The Albanian and I bid a quick farewell to one another under the scorching sun. It was 35 degrees. I got my rucksack and rode my bike to the train station in Bar. Bar, Montenegro's main port city, had a population of fifty thousand. In terms of its history it could be defined as a tourist region but I was so target focused that it didn't occur to me to tour the city.

I paid two Euros for my ticket. I didn't understand if I had to pay for my bike though. Then, holding an ice cream in one hand, water bottle in the other, I found a spot in shade at the train station and sat there observing the ancient building and the town. There wasn't much to look at apart from people who presumably were miserable working in offices without AC's, a kiosk owner probably tired of his monotonous life, a bunch of Anglosaxon tourists who were surprised at the location they ended up at and a dehydrated dog with a blank look on its face. It was clear that Montenegro had a flip side. An aspect that had nothing to do with the images that came up on Google searches of Budva and Kotor…

MONTENEGRO ADVENTURE

*"Use what talents you possess.
The woods would be very silent if no birds
sang there except those that sang best."*

Henry Van Dyke

I was used to hotels or hostels being plain. Or turning out different than how they were marketed on the internet. I was going to stay in a hostel in Podgorica, Montenegro.

This hostel was going to be my home from the second half of July onwards. It was an old consulate building. I arrived there with my backpack, my bike, my shoe bag hanging off it. I stood looking at the huge door, stone walls, the big veranda and the greenest garden ever. Everybody around was eyeing me curiously.

There were two young ladies at the reception and their shift was about to finish as I got there. Also, within a short while I was able to meet all four staff members, including the cleaner and the messenger. Both of the receptionists were called Milica. They knew of my arrival and greeted me much warmer than I had imagined.

The room I was going to stay in was called a 'mixed dorm.' It had bunk beds to host eight and an AC. It let quite a bit of daylight in and looked as if it had been made into two sections. One section had three bunk beds. The other section had a bunk bed, an armchair and was opening up to the bathroom. This hostel's guests were generally tourists who landed in Podgorica late at night for a stopover and continued south later. That's why everybody had checked out when I arrived. The room was vacant, clean and aired out. I chose the section with one bunk bed and threw my rucksack on the upper bunk. Then headed to the shower.

***

I was so beat I slept for hours. When I woke up the sun had already set and all beds were booked. After a few solemn greetings I went down the entrance and chatted with Milica whose actual profession was being a music teacher. I collected some information about the city as well as the country and the hostel. I got confused when a question about my field was raised. Perhaps, I was just tired. Maybe, it was purely because I had no idea of what I was doing. I was able to partially tell my story. I asked Milica where the nearest restaurant was. It was called Pod Volat. I went there.

The first thing that caught my attention in this place called Pod Volat was the prices on the menu. More or less everything was more affordable compared to its counterparts in Italy. Especially the beer… I had a big portion of delicious so-called-kebab-turned-meatballs with butter accompanying it. Following dinner I strolled around the city. My plan was to spot, if any, bike places and small diners that served traditional food. Two hours went by strolling around the city that had been built on both sides of the Morača river. It was a city of barely two hundred thousand people. Everyone was fast asleep in the hostel. I didn't want to wake anybody up but it seemed nearly impossible for me to climb to my upper bunk.

This bunk bed without an access ladder reminded me of my military service days. Back there, our bunk beds didn't have ladders either. We had to climb up the freezing rails so as not to wake the guys in the lower bunks. However, the bunk beds would not be the only things to remind me of those days. Just as I was about to fall asleep the snoring sound coming from the other end of the room shattered my world. My sensitivity toward periodic sounds stopped me from having a good night's sleep. Two-second intervals between each snore had driven me mad. I was in a discomfort the point of gritting my teeth all night.

The next day, I was getting ear plugs.

***

My days at the hostel were more or less the same. I would wake up among seven different people each morning, have breakfast and lunch at the hostel, ride my bike and work on the hostel's new website. Some days I would have less to do in front of the computer. I would help out with the routine work at the hostel. It never felt strange to do all those things while I was barefoot, with a shabby t-shirt and sun faded shorts on. If I were in Turkey I would most definitely hear endless questions and disapproval such as, "Is it proper for a university grad to do cleaning? Make the beds? How is this possible?" But here, nobody judged one another for anything. Everyone was in charge of his or her responsibilities, and that gave me immense contentment.

Some days I would sit in the garden of the hostel and write my book. That way, I could have long chats with hostel guests who came up to me and asked what I was writing. These people, who stayed there either by themselves or with a friend or a lover, became my pals for one day. As time went by, it became so much easier to tell people I know nothing about myself, my wounds, sorrows and how I felt defeated. I found myself listening to their stories as much as they did mine. The nicest thing was I was able to hear a different story each day. For someone like me who likes to observe and gets inspired by the wonder of them, this hostel was a mine rich in gems.

When the work at the hostel slowed down a bit I decided to travel to Belgrade for a few days again with the help of Bla Bla Car but the trip turned out to be not what I had hoped for.

It was after a winding and mostly single lane road when we reached the border at noon together with a few Ukranians. The border police caused me to break out in cold sweat when he asked me innumerable questions for no legitimate reason. It included questions about the cash I was carrying. It made sense since in terms of my distinct nationality amongst the passengers. I finally succumbed to get out of the car and go speak to him. I took out my phone and showed him the screen shots of my articles, magazine clippings and my Instagram account. I was exhausted and nauseous after all the bends but still stood firm and quirky. My aim was to convince him I was not a person of offense. I took a deep breath and went back to the car as the Serbian police stopped dealing with me. He was calm and motionless after I showed him the Euros that one of the Ukraninans tucked in my hand before I had gotten out of the car. As I didn't have the energy to explain to other passengers why I was traveling penniless, I murmured something about having money in my bank account, looked away and didn't lift my head off the car's window until we arrived in Belgrade.

The only thing I knew on my way to Belgrade was the day I was supposed to return to the hostel. I had neither booked a place to stay nor a return trip. My arrangement with the hostel in Montenegro was based on an exchange of services. I wasn't getting paid. I had almost maxed out my savings by then and, in essence, I was in no state to fund this trip. However, I didn't want to resist my urge to travel. I had hit the road thinking, at the very least, a part-time job would be available at some place so I could handle my expenses. When we arrived I walked to the town center and visited several bars with the purpose of finding a job as a scullion. Everyone had some English, one told me the money I would make for two nights' shift. It sounded sufficient enough to buy groceries. I had to crash out in their friend's hostel. It made me happy to find out that their banknotes had Tesla's face on them!

***

Back home, at my parent's house, my relationship to the kitchen was related to my level of hunger. I was never interested in cooking utensils. Whenever I was hungry, I would go get a bite to eat from the fridge. If the dinner is ready, I'd eat it; if it's not, I'd heat up something. If too lazy, I'd eat it cold. Pick up a few fruits if there are some… This was the relationship I had with kitchens.

The first months of living on my own gave me motivation to cook. It slowly decreased. I ordered a lot. Sometimes, my mom would come, cook stuff and leave it for me to consume. Living in the same city with my parents, having a good income and offerings by my ex who was a gastro school graduate had all spoiled me back at home. Now having to stand alone in the kitchen, in other countries and in other cities, became hard. Nevertheless, these were all the basis of a homely feeling. I was forced to learn basic skills I had never developed in life, which was good life experience.

***

Belgrade didn't impress me. I walked about the city during the hours while I was not at the bar's kitchen doing my best. My mind kept sailing back to the days at the military, to the simple jobs like dishwashing.

Certain cities smile at you. Their rivers, parks, people.. they all shine. Even in the rain they smile underneath the umbrella. One doesn't feel beat or distressed in those cities… Whereas others are just like Belgrade. Their most beautiful side of their faces strike as Mona Lisa's. By the time you understand what it's telling you, you realize your numbered days are over and you desert the place taking a few melancholic memories along with you.

My days in Belgrade weren't promising. Perhaps, it was due to the fact that I was tired. I couldn't spare enough time to tour the city or didn't tour it with its locals. It didn't appeal to me at all. The best thing though was to be able to walk outside in the nice weather. That was a big fortune.

***

Dejan was my driver during my return. He was kind, thoughtful and talkative. Not only did he share his snacks and beverages, but he also made a detour to show me Durmitor. I had mentioned my interest in seeing it. Those green summits grander than one another; Tara, the immense second deepest canyon in the world and the Zipline we did along the length of the huge bridge above it all made a big impact on my Durmitor National Park experience. After eating something, we continued our route.

Dejan was on his way to visit his friends in Kotor. As I got to know him better on our drive, I found he was just like me. Keen on living spontaneously, full of surprises, extremely open-minded and a little nut case… He was curious about drinking Nikšićko Pivo in Nikšić. We stopped over and bought some beers. However, either the taste or the percentage of alcohol disappointed him. It tasted like any other beer.

The first thing I did when we eventually connected on Facebook was to check Dejan's birthday. He had been a buddy of mine for a day and it was too hard to say farewell. He was an Aquarius just like me.

***

August's third week, my first month in Montenegro was completed. In my latest trip I had managed to visit cities other than its touristic locations such as Budva and Kotor, and Montenegro had started to feel all too familiar to me. My friends who were after a cheap break contacted me. They wanted to hear my recommendations, came for a visit and looked pretty happy in the pictures they'd sent afterwards.

I worked at the hostel's other branch in Montenegro's port city, Kotor. Climbing up Castle of San Giovanni became a regular activity on my work days. Ascending over a thousand steps, the scenery at the top was truly worth the multiple climbs. People who sold water were as clever as those who emerged out of nowhere on the street when the rain set in. They knew very well where to stand. I noticed the price of water increased as you ascended to the castle. I calculated how much money one could make at the top. During my next visit, I filled up my backpack with bottled water and hurried to the top to sell them before they got too warm. Selling waters was good for my body and my budget. I had felt magnanimously fresh and relieved.

***

A friend of mine, Emre, came to visit me when I was in Bergamo. This time, another friend of mine called Mert came to see me, for a few days, as a surprise. Mert and I had met through cycling connections. When he visited, it was a significantly happy moment. I still remember his black and white bike we breathlessly assembled as soon as he had arrived without even unpacking.

Cash in my pocket just about to get by each day, my bike, sometimes the sea, other times the hills and a good pal… We rode our bikes, stopped at the hill tops and talked for hours and some other times went about discovering Montenegro on foot with our backpacks with Mert, who now works at one of the best advertising agencies in Turkey. I wouldn't worry about anything when Mert was around; he loved risk taking and gave me a touch of his creative aspects in even the simplest chats we had in the best way possible. He was going to leave and I again would be left alone but our memories were so fine that there would be no way something bad could happen in either of our lives from then on.

***

I was on the verge of bewilderment on one of the mornings after finding out Instagram had added Snapchat's story option to its features. After waving goodbye to Mert and started doing routine work at the hostel's branch in Podgorica. A call I received from a +39 number first gave me cramps, then left me in tears and sweet smiles.

It was Nicola calling me. He told me that I would be a good candidate for the marketing department. He referenced the personality test I took, suggested by Rene. Someone called Davide was leaving his position soon. Nicola asked if I would be interested in taking over. He also inquired after what I was doing in Montenegro, what I wanted to do in Italy and about my private life. The call lasted almost twenty minutes and had changed my mood so drastically that I found myself in the garden in need of fresh air, looking blankly at things.

I hugged Milica and the housekeeper Dragana very tightly because I wanted to share and celebrate my good news in the same way everybody did. After all, they were the closest to me right there and then, under the same roof. Dragana was the one who had served me breakfast and lunch at the hostel, made my bed every day, washed my few items of gear a couple of times a week. I dressed my wound after a bike accident on a rainy-day ride and who I sometimes had drinks with together. When Milica and Dragana, they always said they had felt like serving Suleiman the Magnificent in a funny voice and joking sort of way. They told me they would miss me, it brought tears to my eyes. However, I managed to hold back those tears.

Following our phone conversation with Nicola, I received an email containing information about the hiring process. The Blue Card issue I had mentioned to Rene in his office obviously made sense to them. They had decided to apply for a Blue Card for me. In other words, I was going to be transferred to Italy as a skilled immigrant. The procedure wasn't complicated but I had to go to Turkey for paperwork. A Blue Card was considered a legal document both as a residence and work permit. The papers required to be approved were not for one but both permits, which meant extra paperwork.

Upon my departure from Turkey, I had promised myself that I would return only on one condition only. I would be back after I had landed a job. This was, in a way, my oath. As I had mentioned in the previous chapter, I would only go to Italy from Montenegro in the same way I crossed borders to reach from Bergamo to Montenegro. I didn't want to feel defeated. Call it superstition, perhaps determination or even a silly tenacity…Whatever it is, I believe what secured my position during the days I put this ordeal into words, that special thing that kept me in orbit and stopped me from detouring, was this oath.

The company was quite corporate in its affairs. Therefore, an orientation program for the new staff was well in its plan. For this purpose, I was invited to Bergamo for four days in the last week of August. Every piece seemed to have found its place now. My mind was at rest while I was going back to Bergamo. I had acted intuitively and left Schengen states before my ninety-day period had expired and just as I imagined, I was in the need of those few days I'd saved initially just to be on the safe side. If I had stayed my full visa term I could not have participated in the orientation program. Perhaps, some other person would have been hired instead.

When I dropped by the office in my shabby summer outfit and bronzed look, I naturally caught everybody's attention. I cycled to work for orientation days back and forth from the hotel booked by the company on a bike again provided by the company. After office hours, I enjoyed the double bed in my hotel room. No bunk beds, no snoring guests, no stuffiness or stinky smell of a room fully occupied nor shared bathrooms…

None of that any longer.

***

Brand knowledge, promotion of the goods.. I have been acquainted with this. I learned about the general running of things in the company, my position's requirements and many more… I followed a busy schedule for four days. Keeping all a lot of things on my mind, I went straight to the Turkish Consulate in Podgorica. This was after my return to Montenegro from Bergamo. I wanted an attorney to be issued for my dad so he could carry out things on my behalf, along with documentation to be forwarded to the Italian Consulate in Istanbul. There was an email in my inbox awaiting my response to a very-late job offer from a recently opened textile company. I had gladly ignored it, boasted by the grand feeling of having landed a job. I sent all documents enclosing my power of attorney to Turkey. The package delivery to Turkey, the next day, was reasonably priced. It was all thanks to Sevcan, the friend I met at the logistics company during my traineeship while at university (she still worked there). She had a smile and a heart big enough to overcome her illness.

Once again, I truly believed that such people, whose souls roam around the world freely, knew one another at the first instant they saw each other, that they understood one another just by reading between the lines without having had anything serious in common.

***

The owner of the hostel was a fresh mother. Therefore, we hadn't had a chance to meet in person. It was pretty difficult for her to allocate time. When I told her, after my paperwork was resolved in Turkey. My stay in Montenegro was coming to an end. I gathered from her voice that she wasn't smitten. However, she expressed her support for my dreams very kindly.

The longest time I spent between the branches was the central hostel in Podgorica. I didn't like the atmosphere or the staff in others. Nonetheless, this old consulate building left a permanent mark. There had been some bad memories as I recall. For example, it proved impossible to go to sleep some days due to carbon dioxide levels in the room. Everyone besides me slept soundly. They were visitors of the country who'd get tired at the end of each day. I didn't get tired so easily during the day including those when I rode my bike. When my sleep deprivation hit its peak, I went down to the reception desk. My purpose was to check if there were any vacant double beds. Rooms with double beds, allocated to couples, were the most expensive at the hostel. Some days they would stay vacant. I brought my pillow and sneaked in to secretly sleep in a room with a double bed. It was until the housekeeping hour; the bed was made before I left so neatly. No one noticed somebody was sleeping in it. I was only after double beds in regards to those rooms. From time to time, a place between walls with several beds could become the most uncomfortable corner. Much worse was there than those tiny tents on a rugged terrain.

In spite of all that, I loved this temporary home. I tried to concentrate on the many delightful things it offered. At the commune breakfast each morning, I introduced myself over and over again. A character straight out of *50 First Dates*; where he'd hang the washing out in its garden and walk barefoot on grass. The idea of parting depressed me. It meant more than a hostel building. It was a magical home that embraced me. Especially, since I was going through the most important breaking point in my life.

The place evokes the sweet smell of summer, freedom, an inspiration to the words in my book. Plus, a third ear to the stories told by each new traveler... It meant the petite French girl whom I chased after until we reached Kotor. I held her hand tight to the top of the castle and kissed breathlessly. It meant two huge turtles and a bunch of drunk guys brought into the room at midnight trying to make me eat. They made me think they were offering watermelons. The scar that would perpetually stay on my right knee actually meant my bike uniform had become unwearable.

***

After I received confirmation from the Italian Consulate in Istanbul, I decided to join the bike tour in The Dardanelles organized by some friends. It was one of the two big holidays in Turkey. Now that I had a job, I could visit home. Felt like a double festivity... Time to box my bike; which I wasn't able to manage back in Montenegro.

A small but well-organized bike shop staff in Podgorica, in return for my support for their social media accounts as a consultant, were kind enough to pack my bike neatly in a box. They made it as if it were one of their own. Additionally, it was delivered to the hostel a day before my departure. My night's sleep that day was so uneventful and uninterrupted. I heard no snoring nor sniffed a stink...

When I boarded the flight, I had finalized my work in Montenegro on the date I had promised, gulped down Montenegro's Ottoman-like food. I never skipped the famous grilled calamari stuffed with cheese. Consumed too many beers only because beer was cheap... Had numerous disagreements with its careless drivers, met its broad-shouldered women, listened to calls to prayers at sunsets... I was tanned and ready to start my new life.

This time I was going to Istanbul not to take roots but to break away from them.

SECOND SIEGE OF BERGAMO

My parents welcomed me warmly apart from my dad whining about the consulate paperwork and its cost. My mom cooked my favorite dishes. My dad had missed me. He would never admit that. Our retrieval with my five cats was special. I didn't get out of the house the first few days to spend time with them. There wasn't much I was homesick about anyways. I just wanted to get some rest. Maybe, have some fun with my friends and prepare my mental state for the new job.

On sunny days, I met with friends from Kadıköy, Moda and Caddebostan Three beautiful neighbourhoods in the Asian side of Istanbul… I popped into my favorite restaurants, ate good food. After a separation of four months, I hopped on my bike again. Nothing had really changed, nothing special that moved me…

I got aggressive against drivers who failed to drive. I was wary of them and just rode past them. Before, as I left the traffic behind and headed for the bike track, I would get flustered with the sea air hitting me. Now the only thing I did was to look for a spot on the grass to sit nonchalantly. Once, I used to think I had a predicament. Now, none was of any interest to me.

Perhaps I had lost my sympathy toward this city. It became dispirited; because back then, I thought I was a permanent subject in Istanbul. Now, it was all but a transient. Nothing beckoned me there.

***

Riding a bike in the early hours of the day, watching poetic sunrises, gaining at least double the amount of calories.. That's how I like starting the day. I genuinely believe that one burns calories when the food is organic… The sea, the sand, the sun and some ice cream helps…

Vacation in Assos cured my wounded existence. Assos is a small, elegant village on the Aegean cost, near Gallipoli. Once, it was Aristotle's home, where he wrote some of his work. At least, that's what they sell to the tourists. For me, it is a beautiful coastal city with healing powers and an amazing sea.

I had both fulfilled my longing for being with many of my friends, which

I couldn't have back in Bergamo. I got to ride my bike and gazed around. The idea of not hearing Turkish language in the next chapter of my life uplifted. It is not that I hated the language, but I wanted more and a new beginning. I'd be in a new land. For now, the moment deserved to be cherished. What a coast... Living the life I wanted to live and acting the way I wanted to act had its price. Just before I came to Assos, I met someone with the same dreams of living abroad as did I. Someone whose smile, look and touch felt amazing to my soul from the first moment... What we shared together made it possible to soothe me most fittingly in those last days before I left Turkey. The combination of fury, anguish and yearning bewildered me back then. I had felt a tight connection to her until the last day of my stay. Hence, I stayed connected beyond that period into the first phase in Italy. It was perhaps as a consequence of the extreme sentimentality taken over me back then. Perhaps, she had the same problematic family bonds just like I did. In the course of my decision to leave Turkey, there had been no one I wanted to take with me. Yet, when it came to her, every time I thought of the things I would be facing in the coming weeks. I craved her, wanted her next to me.

***

Days were numbered. I ended up in Istanbul. I remembered setting aside the luggage I'd left in Bergamo when I traveled to Montenegro from Bergamo as a lucky charm. Thus, I had decided not to take too much stuff with me. Each time mom kept saying, "You will need this, too, listen to your mom!" and bringing more stuff to me. I had to remind her that I was only moving to another city, not joining the military. Though she still managed to shove in bits and pieces here and there.

Suitcase, backpack, documents and a boxed bike... I was now ready to leave. Following the same footsteps before, I wanted to go visit the famous tarot card reader to hear more about my future. She mentioned that I would dwell on money mainly through two channels. I would dissemble my life only to rebuild it again and again. I would eventually achieve success. My spirits had risen.

Nevertheless, in between my readings, I was prompted by her hinting that I would possibly be back home in October. Any October, without stating the year... I felt as if I had been hit by a blow. When she noticed my face started to sulk, she immediately changed the course of the reading.

I was so unprepared to hear anything about my return that I didn't want a story with a return theme in it; be it my tarot reading. There was only one topic I was focused on: going to Italy and staying there.

***

This time the journey was uneventful. I checked in my suitcases peacefully and went through security checks eating junk food. It might be related to either the fact that I was going to a city I already knew or because I would be staying at a hotel for a month booked and paid by the company. However, I wasn't stressed at all on my way to the airport, on the apron and throughout the flight. I was feeling the same as I would when starting any new job.

The small hotel I was going to stay was quite a bit off Bergamo and a kilometer to the office. Roberto collected me from the airport. We drove to the hotel in twenty minutes. After helping me out with my bags he left me on my own.

The hotel was covered in orange wallpapers and had laminate flooring. In each step, the floor creaked. I didn't care much about it. Every corner was full of old furniture, patterned giant window panes and huge door knobs. These details were also present in my room. They made me feel as if I was in another era. After I put away a few items in a huge chest, what I supposed to be sort of a wardrobe, I rested for a bit in the double bed in this presumably single room. Soon the smell of wet soil after rain filled the air in the room through the shutters. My lungs expanded. Everywhere smelled of nature. Moments passed and I started losing connection with time and space. My eyes seemed to have stopped transmitting what they saw to my mind. As I lay there I felt my heart beat in part of my body. Minutes later I got up, pulled out a few allen keys and went next to my boxed bike I'd left at the entrance of the hotel.

Il Borgo's managers Simona and Roberto were parents to a son in his early twenties. They saw me attending to my bike in the rain and told me dinner would be ready shortly. It was hard to resist the smell. I was starving but I had to get ready for my bike ride. In half an hour my bike was up and running. I took some photos of it. I then parked my bike in the hotel's storeroom. I joined the couple for dinner.

Over dinner I briefly shared with them information about Istanbul, Turkey, about writing, bikes and my new job. I was very pleased I was going to be together with Simona and Roberto during my stay there in the next month. They were very kind and considerate. Their level of English was better than my Italian. Much of the conversation was carried out in English. After over an hour of chatting at the dinner table I asked for permission to go up to my room. I had arrived on a Sunday for a much affordable air ticket and the next day was my first day at work. I wanted to go to sleep early and wake up refreshed.

***

I would be seeing Simona each morning; she was ready to offer toast, apricot jam and coffee for breakfast. Her hair had silver highlights and a couple of shades of blue which suited her joyful character and it felt great to see her smiling face. I had started my first work day in Italy at a place that didn't belong to me, having breakfast prepared by someone I had never met in my life before.

The first few days in my new job were pretty hectic and exciting. Everything was new. Responsibilities, tasks, people, bikes, my email address, my computer, passwords, desk, notebook and many other stuff… However, I reminisced about certain, unaltered things from my past. Two weeks hadn't passed when I witnessed forlorn attempts of colleagues. They breathed in the corporate air but found themselves and their skills inadequate. Their solutions were to suck up to their bosses. I was sad to realize the nature of people in such a pretty building. If this beautifully designed office had hosted the right kind of people to work, it would turn into a wonderful working environment.

I had to stay at the hotel for a month as the company declared the hotel my temporary residing address. In other words, I was to spend my first month here in a godforsaken place and commute from there. I was legally bound to do so. I was on autopilot, went to work in crappy weather, dealt with never-ending emails and mismatched tasks. Then, I went back to my hotel room. Frequency of public transportation was scarce as the town where the hotel was quite far off the city of Bergamo. In the event of catching the bus, it took me an hour to get to the center because the bus had to stop at small villages around the city.

There were other nationalities at the office, like me, who were not Italian. Bence was my first buddy. A young engineer from Hungary, he helped me on a lot of issues. He had a pessimistic side to his character, looked displeased about certain things he had been asked to do but worked very hard.

He generally left the office late and did not complain. He wanted to get himself into a discipline of work as this was his first job. As for the British guy whom I had a good dialogue with back in August during orientation week, he wasn't there anymore. Bence told me that the British guy was a nice colleague and one of the 3 or 4 guys in the office, including himself, who rode bikes.

My position at work had required collaborations with colleagues from various departments. After my initiation, according to the schedule of training, I was handed. I had to go visit these people on the exact days and times. Since nobody had time, it became difficult. Everyone kept postponing what they were supposed to teach me. This being the case, I would go back to the hotel without having learned anything at work. I didn't have a car to jump in and drive around, it would become boring. I'd go to sleep.

My unease increased as time went on. So, did my workload that had never been stated within my job description… I was obligated to do so. My motivation to finish those tasks decreased rapidly to the contrary. As I didn't like the people I worked with, I went to the office a little later each day and looked for ways to leave early. I was about a month into my job when my supervisor held a meeting with me saying he wanted to review my responsibilities. I was miles away, I don't remember even now what he had said in that meeting. He'd kept showing figures and definitions in a chart reflecting his tension in his voice. He seemed to take his job seriously in a fanatic way. When, at the end of the meeting he asked if I wanted to go through the revised list of responsibilities. I had said I didn't want to and these weren't what I had come there for. The new chores did not involve creativity or any use of brain function. Those aspects were covered by the owners of the company. Just like my supervisor, the people in marketing did no more than carry out instructions without contribution.

I realized I wasn't going to last long in this office. Thus, I started communicating as much as I could with those who could teach me something. Whenever I got hold of Simone I would bombard him with lots of questions. He had worked at Campagnolo, a brand I admired very much, for many years. He lived in Padova. Therefore, came into the office only twice a week and he worked from home for the remainder of the time. Even though he was under a time constraint, aware of my will to learn, he never refused to answer any question I had.

I found myself counting days. It was likely that I wasn't doing anything. Nothing motivated me, I genuinely did not like my job. In spite of this, I had made up my mind about renting a flat, willfully acknowledging the fact that my expenses would increase. Finding a flat didn't take me too long. I found a condo across from the bar I stopped for a coffee after a ride. Together with Bence we gathered all my stuff. He had a car. I checked out of the hotel and moved into the flat. I tried to personalize my new home in the heart of Bergamo as much as possible. I furnished the house and spent that week getting used to my new route. Walk to the bus stop, get on a bus, spend an hour of commute half awake, get off the bus and go work… Following a bike ride on the weekend with a British guy who was looking for a new job, it felt great to go back home instead of that hotel room in the outskirts of Bergamo. Though Monday syndrome had already started showing its effects from Saturday night; going to work on Monday felt like torture.

When on Monday, even before I had a chance to read my emails, Nicola told me at the end of the phone line he wanted to see me. It was obvious we were going to part ways, I was expecting it. He had another manager with him during our meeting and wanted to hear what my thoughts were. If I had told him I wanted to stay anyway and maybe, I would be more careful from then on. I could have stayed. The purpose of the meeting was obviously an official warning. Anyhow, I appeared so unwilling that both of the parties decided to cut it short. Friday would be my last day in the office. When I came out of the conference room I was quiet for about ten minutes like a child who had just fallen but showed no sign of it. With one hand cupped my cheek, my eyes on the screen blankly, I tried finishing the day's work on the computer.

I couldn't even enjoy my new home now that I was waiting for my unemployment. My work visa was valid for a year. With all documentation I had collected, I had applied for a Blue Card and booked an interview for my residence permit. I had met the terms that were legally binding for me to be here, so, there was no room for panic, I thought. The Italian bureaucracy, in all its likelihood and very similar to that of Turkey's, had granted me an interview for January. I had applied for one in October. This was no surprise because my residence permit interview back in 2008. When I first came to Siena, my appointment was booked for January. I had brought my documents with me from school then and had convinced myself that everything was under control. The penny dropped. I realized that whatever documentation I would be taking with me would have no validity. They were all work related and the residence permit on my Blue Card was to be issued based on the contract submitted on a stamp on my passport. There and then I started to feel something real. It hurt.

***

Confrontation of this fact brought me to the conclusion that it was meaningless to work effortlessly in that office until Friday. I was not going to be employed there. I had to focus my energy on myself and what to do instead. Nicola took this decision well and let me go. I didn't bid farewell to anyone except Bence, whom I heard later left the following month also. I packed my cup that had a funny illustration of myself with my Pinarello bike, which I had to sell the frame of in order to pay the upcoming rent. Also, Socrates's photo, one of my cats in Istanbul, I left the office.

I became flatmates with the British guy who left the company before me. I didn't want to lose my mind out of loneliness and end up making consecutive mistakes in panic.

The British guy's story was very similar to mine. He had moved to Italy after a choking kind of life in London and started riding his bike here. It reincarnated his soul. Now he was spending his days not regretting anything about yet leaving another job of six months behind. A job he had landed through a Polish friend of his.

It didn't take long for two unemployed immigrants like us to get used to one another. We were able to share between us the house chores. There was no tension around the house as both of us were quiet types. A usual melancholy of being unemployed, from time to time, could be sensed. Nothing bothered me about him except the intense smell of garlic around the flat when he cooked.

December came and it brought with its cold weather. I didn't go out much except for basic shopping needs except for hopping on our bikes with my housemate, from time to time.

I did some research on particular websites and forums. With my visa, in the event of being unemployed for longer than three months, I'd be deported. However, I doubted it was inspected and conducted properly. Still, I needed to be on alert. Moreover, I had to find a way to cover the cost of house expenses, I managed surviving by borrowing money from friends. I visited Andrea to see if he could find a job for the British guy. This time for myself but to no avail. The next day I met with Enrico. He had left Bianchi store and opened his own place upstate. He would have an opportunity to have me work with him in the months ahead. Unfortunately, I couldn't stay for that reason. Then I thought of that email from the textile company that I hadn't responded to. I couldn't just write to them after all this time.

The whole process of job hunting was back to square one. I started sending out my revised resume to other brands.

***

New Year's Eve was as dismal as the one I spent during my military service eating strawberry waffles. I rapidly started losing weight after my bike was stolen. It was three days after new year's. I lost my appetite. My housemate was trying his best to feed me. I dropped down from the weight I held back in Istanbul from: 85 kilograms to 77. I had kept on being 85 for a long time.

I was in the state of my life where I couldn't afford bags of grocery shopping. Nor could I eat out often enough. Along my stolen bike, nutrition had become the last thing on my mind. During this period when I weighed 67 kilos, each time I attempted to stand up my vision went black and my tongue was tingling. I had no energy left. Playing the new version of Football Manager was the only habit of mine at that time. Sometimes I tried reading or writing. At night, I remember, falling asleep wasn't easy even though I had gone to bed early. Some nights I couldn't get any sleep because of hunger.

Andrea knew how much my stolen bike meant to me, despite our short acquaintance. He was well aware that I had sold my Pinarello's frame. I had no access to any bike. For that reason, the next day straight after the procedures at the police station, he provided me with a temporary bike from Stelbel via Cicli Corsa. Looking like a child in need of consolation facing him, I had first sniffled. I wiped my tears, then got on my new bike and rode home. I lost my job, my bike. I was hungry and concerned about how I was going to pay next month's rent.

Even though I had been robbed off my bike, my intention was to continue living in Bergamo and find work. Needless to say, the situation was not financially sustainable any longer. I tried my luck by sending an email to Alessandro. He was a British guy I had met at a bicycle fair. He never called again. The job he had mentioned was already taken.

The company was located in a town called Bassano del Grappa. It was approximately an hour from Venice and with a population of forty thousand. They were looking for someone for the marketing department. A few emails and a phone call guaranteed me for a job interview. I was confirmed to have the interview on the day just before my birthday.

I asked Alessandro to send me an official letter stating they were in the process of recruitment. I had a scheduled interview for my residence permit several days later. It was mandatory for me to have a residence permit.

Questura's tiny waiting room was chock a block, the majority of the people were Africans. I started waiting for my turn among expecting mothers and their babies in tow, coughing kids, men speaking loudly and a few volunteer translators. Essentially, everyone had a scheduled appointment though the amount of work wouldn't let it run smoothly. I parted ways with the warm radiator's touch and hurried toward the partition when my name was announced after forty minutes.

The police officer, having had a quick look at me from the other side of the glass, told me my documents were in good shape. had to wait for another round to have my fingerprints scanned. A few minutes passed and I was called back. This time, I was directed to another office through a door. My height, weight and vision data were recorded, my fingerprints were scanned and, without any interrogation, I was sent home with a request to collect my card in a month.

Not a question about how long I had been unemployed, nor any information regarding I'd left my job… I didn't have to deal with anything. Perhaps my fair hair and shaved face, perhaps my proper attire or maybe my thorough papers… Nobody had asked me any questions.

That was it. It was over.

***

I had to borrow the money for the bus fares from my flat mate for my meeting with Alessandro. We were going to meet at a restaurant in Vicenza on January 24. I had a very limited budget. When Alessandro had reminded me not to throw away the receipts and reimbursed me. I was both embarrassed and pleased. I was pleased because part of me insisted that this was how it should be.

Alessandro gave me a tour of the company and presented me a t-shirt with the company's logo on it. While I was putting the t-shirt on he was cheering, "Welcome to the team!" I had felt like a football player kissing the club's flag. That photo is still posted on my Instagram account. My bike in the front, me, wearing that t-shirt and one more object invisible in the picture: the thought cloud "what the hell am I doing here?"

The recent positive outcomes in my life had me start eating better and riding my bike more toward the end of January. Without minding the cold weather, I rode my blue steel bike almost every day and posted more often on social media. The result was an increase in the number of interactions by my followers regarding the bike that I had borrowed. It was a nice surprise I had welcomed into my miserable life. The same increase must obviously have been observed in the number of emails also at Stelbel. I received an affirmative response from Andrea about my proposal of a bike frame custom-made for me. I had my own wheels and groupset. It was a mutually profitable arrangement. This was the best news I received considering the whole year.

***

I had invited Burak quite often to come visit me in Bergamo; I hadn't seen my friend in a long time. However, he couldn't spare any time to do this; neither before my Montenegro trip nor during the period when I was earning money and my pocket was full.

His first available time slot to visit was early February. My flat mate was in London with his parents then and I was home, penniless, waiting to hear from the company about my possible employment. Even though Burak and I didn't go around too much, we managed to have a good time together. At least we tried to attribute positive affirmations between ourselves in relation to life. We kept reminding each other of what we had achieved, let our thoughts linger on what we could do better and configured the next required steps. There weren't any Freudian couches left. At the very least, we were not in Istanbul, we were still able to make the most of Burak's visit. There hadn't been any progress about my new job nor of my lost bike. It was as if life had halted. Burak was a person who knew me very well, so he tried to keep me calm.

On the same day, I said farewell to Burak, swore at the lousy weather in Bergamo, went to pick up my residence permit and dropped a line to Alessandro. My aim was to inform my landlord of the date I had planned to move out. Also, to arrange a vehicle accordingly. However, his response was overwhelming. He said that another interview had to be scheduled in which all company members participated. "Well, why, then, had he acted as if I was hired?"

I had to do the same commute; visited the same place, introduced myself all over again. I was pretty reluctant, and had perceived the disorganized nature in the company. On the other hand, I was trying to be well-behaved as I needed to earn money.

When I returned to Bergamo I received a phone call from Nicola. After the interview the company had called my former employer for a reference check. I guess I must have thanked Nicola at least ten times during our phone conversation for providing them with positive feedback about me.

My landlord Lorenzo tried to find some people who could help me move to Bassano in return for a reasonable price. It was a challenge to find something that fit my budget. In fact, I didn't have much to move. If I had to carry everything myself, it would take me two train journeys. That would turn out to be costly. My final solution was to call Andrea. Andrea told me he would be driving the company's van to Padova, a city close to Bassano that week, he noted the date I had to move. I hung up.

***

When my phone rang the next day Andrea had not one but two good news. First, my bike's frame was ready. Secondly, he had managed to organize his drive for the same date as my move. That evening I went to his garage and started watching my bike being put together. I was overjoyed about the bike. However, I felt a bit down as well. I wanted to stay in Bergamo and work with him in this tiny workplace. Instead, I had to go to Bassano. I installed the tyres onto my new bike. I hugged Andrea and left.

On the day of my move, I was ready to leave Bergamo with all my belongings stuffed into my bike box and tyre bags, my suitcase, rucksack and my new red bike. I chatted with Andrea on the way and half slept. After my second interview at the new company I had an opportunity to tour the city and look for houses with a realtor. I knew what lay ahead. Still, it felt exciting to be at the start of living in a new surrounding.

I unloaded my belongings. I set them in a corner on a nearby street, said farewell to Andrea and waited for the realtor to bring the keys to the new flat. Five minutes passed and the realtor came with the landlord. I took the keys, tried to make small talk with my new landlord who didn't speak any word of English. I carried all my stuff inside and threw myself on the mattress without taking my shoes off.

I had come to realize once again, after my struggle with the landlord, I needed to learn some level of Italian. A month from that date would mark the first anniversary of my Italian adventure. I, unfortunately, were never able to dwell on the correct resources to enroll myself in Italian lessons. As my preferred communication with people was in English, I didn't learn any Italian. One of the requirements of acquiring Carta d'identità, the Italian ID Card, was an A2 level of Italian. I hadn't done anything for that yet.

I wrote an email to Andrea expressing how grateful I was of his continued support. I would always be there to help if he needed me. This was a long message because, in between the lines, I had also mentioned I wanted to work with him. If he should call, I would be more than happy to leave my current position and go back and work with him. I went out as soon as I sent the email. I got used to this cute Italian town with its small-scale squares, bridge, happy faces and streets with whiffs of Prosecco in no time.

***

Valentina became my first friend in Bassano. We had connected on Instagram; she lived quite near. Some weeknights we used to eat Veneto cuisine and then tour wine houses in the vicinity. On weekends, when we had the chance, we used to go to her cottage in Alta Badia at the skirts of Dolomites in northern Italy and fill our lungs with fresh air. I had warmed up to this new place, even intended to adopt a kitten, but first, I had to be more in touch with the pulse of the company and be sure of my colleagues and myself.

I discovered new routes and mountain tops on my bike. The intensity of my feelings in the direction of getting to know new colleagues and new assignments was about to be tired out. At the very start of my second month I had visited Germany on business and shortly after my return. I gave a presentation to a large crowd at a dealers meet. The topic was effective use of digital marketing and social media in the bicycle industry. I felt what I learned from there and what I contributed to them was sufficient for me. I more or less had an idea about what the future might bring.

I visited Turkey briefly toward the end of April. I sold some of my now too-large cycling kits, my old mobile phone and shoes via the internet. I made very little money on those. I left the remaining cycling gear at my friend Emirhan's recently opened shop so he could give them away to charity. My intention at first was to sell whatsoever cycling items I no longer used. This way, I could raise enough capital to publish my first book. Yet, leaving those items at Emirhan's shop sounded like the best decision to make at the time. I knew there were cyclists who needed such things and I wanted to be the one to serve that purpose.

On my return to Bassano del Grappa, I realized that working eight hours a day, commuting to work with 19-year-old hip-hop enthusiast Lorenzo whose father ran a bike shop in Todi, seeing the same people on the streets each and every day, and drinking Campari Spritz in the same bars won't take my anywhere.

I decided to desert the town. In essence, apart from its close proximity to The Dolomites and Monte Grappa, the town didn't hold any special characteristics to it. Its tininess had started to take a toll in me. If I'd had a car I would have stayed a little longer and driven around the locations I mentioned above thoroughly. However, in a town of forty thousand people, I neither had the money to spend nor time to waste, unless I went to Venice on the weekends. My second job taught me that the bicycle industry doesn't make people rich.

Following my decision, I first contacted my former landlord Lorenzo. Then I contacted the British guy. Lorenzo had said the flat would be vacant after the first week in June but the news I received from the Brit wasn't great. He had started working with Andrea and now was living by himself. I tried to shake off the impact of hearing the news. It made me feel like I was in an abyss. I broke off with the company by letting them know I would be leaving at the end of May. And somehow managed to dismiss a few weak attempts to convince me to stay. Thus, knowing I would not be strong enough to say no to the owner of the company had I answered his call. I went on gathering my stuff and ignored the call.

I knew right from the start that I couldn't continue working there because of certain setbacks. Just like I did in my first job. So, I had saved every penny I earned there. I had not spent money on any luxuries items and avoided buying clothes unless it was a necessity. Also, as the flat was refurbished I didn't need to make any purchases. Ultimately, I was able to save a little over a quarter of my three salaries in total.

***

Veneto region in Italy is renowned for its Prosecco wineries. For this reason, Prosecco prices in such cities as Padova, Treviso, Venice and Bassano del Grappa have been low and varieties are plenty. All these varieties of Prosecco, some famous big brands and some small enterprises. I could easily be found almost in every little wine corner around the city called Enoteca in Italian. There was one of those just across from where I lived. I had taken to tasting a new brand each time I passed it by. As Prosecco is so much favored by the Italians and can be consumed any time during the day. Thanks to the owner, Alfredo, a very sweet guy, he let me taste at least two different brands with no cost at all. I reached a mastery of distinguishing one from the other.

I asked Alfredo for his help a few days before moving out whether he could arrange a large cab for me to take me back to Bergamo. From my A1 level Italian, I understood he was bargaining. Next in the list was getting my stuff together. One of my suitcases was in terrible condition. Nevertheless, I did not want to make a purchase for a three-hour ride in a cab. That size of a suitcase cost almost a hundred Euros. My solution was to secure the full suitcase in duct tape once I packed everything. I was finally ready for my, hopefully, last departure. Once more this time, the bags carrying my tyres were starring in this movie. I carried my bags out one by one, gulped down the "farewell drink" Alfredo had given me (sort of a similar Turkish tradition of throwing a bowl of water before a traveler sets off on his journey) I gazed for the last time at the cute streets of Bassano, a city I only cherished for a season as a worker, not an inhabitant. I started a cab ride with a driver who didn't know a word of English.

***

When I got back to the siege of Bergamo after a three-month break, Lorenzo met me in all his hospitality and helped me carry my stuff up to my lodgings. The house was in the same shape as the Ryanair stewardesses who had rented the place. I spent a good deal of time at home while I was in Bassano. So, I managed to get things running pretty quickly after a good clean and sorting-out.

Having spent a few quiet days at home I had to go to Bormio. I was supposed to meet friends there as we had promised while on vacation in Assos a year before to participate in a race that would take place in Bormio. We had a rental awaiting us there. All of them were easy to get on with, like-minded, fun guys. It was also great that we were all going our own way during the vacation. We might as well call it a bike holiday. We seemed to have found a way to release the stress build-up both in Bassano and Istanbul on climbing tracks. One day in Gavia, next in Mortirolo and on another day in Stelvio… As we crowned the days we pedaled like crazy with awesome dinners I came to recognize the feeling that I had really missed sitting at crowded tables.

Those dinners were a true catalyst for me to understand once more why Italians had the saying, "Those who eat together, stay together." I never had a chance to sit at such packed dinner tables after that.

I bid farewell to my friends in Bormio. I didn't know when I'd see them next. So I hopped on a train to Bergamo, to my flat, in the hopes that the smell of bleach had already evaporated. In four months, it would be my first anniversary in Bergamo as an immigrant. I wanted to renew my residence permit. Although, if I wanted to build a life in Italy, I needed to find a solid job. Going back to Turkey wasn't an option. If things didn't go well, I could take another chance in Montenegro and keep looking for work while I was there.

"You won't work in a small company. You won't work in a big company. You won't work in a corporate company or at a family business. Where do you work?"

My dad was scolding me on the phone. He was right but a stumping phone call was the last thing I needed. So, I didn't let it linger. I listened to him and nodded. Then I ended the conversation, quite adamant to do what I believed would be the best thing to do.

My dad never believed in me from the start. This, at least, was how he made me feel. I will never forget that one day when there was going to be an exam to determine the level of students entering fourth grade for middle school preparations. We, students, took a test of one hundred questions in which we were required to fill in the correct answers. They were organized by private training centers. We all waited for the results of this strenuous test. There had been a parent-teacher conference straight after to exchange ideas. The review of the test took place and they went through the year-end academic results. At the parents meeting, my dad told me, "Well, we'll see, won't we, when we get the results!" I was an active and impish boy; but never an underachiever. That's why I couldn't understand why my dad had expressed such a thing. My teacher must have noticed the same thing in what my dad had mentioned so she felt she had to correct him by kindly reminding him of my high scores in the mock exams at the school. Hence, when the results were announced we had found out I was eligible for a full scholarship at a highly recognized training institution. I was not sure if my dad was at all happy because he then had questioned why I hadn't scored 100 instead of 90. All in all, if there were one party to have seen what mattered most. That certainly wasn't me.

It took me a long time to process my daddy issues.

***

I began reminding myself one by one the motives I'd had before coming here.

"Why did I come here?" To finish my book.

First and foremost, I had to handle that part. My book was fully written, I had to have it published. It was after I posted on social media when Mr. Kadir Aydemir, owner of a publishing house famous for their support for budding writers, contacted me to tell me he wanted to see my book. It was as if he believed in it being a success. Thus, he expressed his interest in publishing it without me having any costs.

A few days passed and I received the good news: My book was going to be published! Months of anticipation in a state of stress and agony had finally turned out to bear its fruit. In all my life's uncertainty, the book was going to be the only solid thing. I would get to keep the money I had set aside to publish my book. This situation had eradicated the urgency of my job searches in Bergamo. I was more independent in moving forward with better substantial plans.

I wanted to go on a short break first. One evening when I found myself at Milano Malpensa Airport. After a day of thinking solely about the sun, sea and sand, I turned up in Amsterdam. It is the twist. Then, I went to Berlin and after, to Prague. My budget was drained. I came back to Bergamo at an unconventional time on a cheap flight.

Traveling always worked favorably for me. Each time I realize I am wavering, I search for an alternate perspective. On that matter, I live off the grid for a while and regroup. I believe existing in new surroundings is quite beneficial in clearing clogged arteries. Also, it lets the train of thoughts flow effortlessly. Depending on my mood, I travel sometimes idly. On some occasions, I do a lot of research about the places I go to.

When I returned to Bergamo I felt there was something amiss at home. A void, the absence of a living being, a beating heart… I spent my last years in Istanbul among cats and felt the growing emptiness about the lack of them in Italy. Unfortunately, my income wasn't sufficient to take care of a cat, to offer a proper home to it.

Even though I knew I couldn't have one straight ahead, the need of adopting a pet had made me feel content. I took it as a sign of longing for a stable home. Adopting a cat was a symbol of stability.

***

In order to transform into a more substantial life, I knew I had to do something about it. If it were only in my wishes, it wasn't going to be realized. Now, I was determined to move forward toward a singular target. Once again, I had to remind myself of the reason for moving to Italy. Yes, I wanted to work at a company in Italy with a focus on the bicycle industry. I had the correct contact list for this. After an evening out with Andrea drinking beer when, this time, we talked about what he wanted to do. I had already expressed my wish to work with him on numerous occasions. I found out how the British guy started working with him. One of Andrea's employees left and the other one was about to leave. He offered me a job to start in August.

In this period between the end of June and beginning of August I contacted no company for a job. The only thing I did was to ride bike. I wanted to keep close contact with only the people I loved and avoided those who would drag me into their swamp. They were bullying me by asking the questions: "So, what will you do now?" I know it wasn't well intended, it had the purpose of taking me down. I , who had quit his job in Bassano and returned to Bergamo, had first traveled, then rode my bike every waking day of the week. I went back home to see my parents and finally had arrived in Bergamo and enjoyed the newly-discovered pool.

The time I spent at home felt like a cure. It was a process of restoring myself, enjoying loved ones and cherishing my cats I had immensely missed.

***

As promised, Andrea contacted me the first week in August. He introduced the rest of the company to me, though I knew all of them, and briefed me about what I was going to be responsible for. Those were the most special moments in Bergamo for me as I was in a state of elation to be doing things together. Especially, under the same roof with the people I pedaled with.

Cicli Corsa was a small but promising company managed by Andrea and his partner Alessandro. It had already incorporated a strong brand like Stelbel into its realm. There was a lot to do and all these, under digital marketing, either scripted or visual, were directly related to everything about the end-user experience. Therefore, my work would provide feedback, positive or negative, in a short period. It's a truth we all acknowledged so far, I was not a patient person. I left the meeting in the office quite content with my new job description and headed to my favorite ice cream shop in Bergamo; La Romana.

Having completed two weeks in the office, I embarked on finding myself a fluffy roommate and started checking out websites for pets. I aimed to finalize this with my first salary. I checked pet ads daily, sending messages to the ones I liked and impatiently pressing the refresh button to see if I had a response. Almost a month after, on a Facebook page I followed, I found a three-and-a-half-month-old greyish white kitten, who I would later be calling Zelda. She was looking around her curiously.

When I brought her home with me the same day with all her stuff, I wanted Zelda to act as my shackles in Bergamo. I voluntarily placed her around my ankles. I wanted her to diminish me so I couldn't blast off each time I got angry about something. It also had the purpose to force me to stay grounded. I wanted to make my decisions calmly. It took us less than a week to get used to one another and by the first days of September, we were already inseparable as sleep buddies and life partners.

***

Toward mid-fall I started private Italian lessons with a friend of Andrea's. I stopped continuing them after several sessions, I couldn't get into that. I had decided to do this by myself. The season was slowly turning and I was riding my bike less each day. I now had more free time to study Italian. I knew sooner or later, I had to take the aptitude test for immigrants that the

Italian government offered. If I succeeded in that test I would be eligible for an Italian ID card. That also meant indefinite residence permit. I wanted to start the citizenship process from the date of my first approved residence permit.

I got myself together, applied for the Italian language exam and began waiting for the big day. My studies came to a brief halt when I had to travel to Taiwan on my own for a competition. However, I was quite motivated and ready to catch up from where I had left off when I got back. I was thrown into a new routine those days. I went to work. I came back home in the evening and studied Italian and went to bed. All I could think of was to pass the test. I never spared any time for activities other than playing with Zelda or going on short bike rides. At some point, my focus was out of sorts as my book Cloud Factory was published. But, actually, it was an event that had had an impact on my life back in Turkey. Though here in Italy, now, I had to fully concentrate on my life. My efforts of utilising Italian and listening to it being spoken at work as much as possible were paid off. I was overjoyed with the result of my test a multitude of times. I had achieved a much better performance than I had expected. So, it had been a splendid closing to the fall for me. I was ready to welcome 2018 with no doubts on my mind.

***

Streets in Bergamo were already getting started to be decorated for Christmas, Christmas trees were placed in all squares in the city, big or small, when I decided to let go of my last bike in Istanbul to pay off my gas bill and a few purchases I needed to make for my house. I was upset to be saying goodbye to the bike I ardently put together back in 2013. At the same time, I really needed the cash I'd receive from that bike. After all, that bike was the last connecting dot to my days as I had initially decided what I owned should not have owned me. My hesitation proved justified and I was able to sell my bike almost for its original value at an auction.

I paid the gas bill and I breathlessly ended up at a mall upstate in a shopping frenzy together with every Italian. The shopping mall was called Orio and it reminded me of my days in Istanbul because there were people everywhere. It was as if every citizen from around Bergamo had flowed in there. At least my shopping list was brief and I was not going to waste any more time. According to my plans, I was supposed to leave the mall with a TV and a PlayStation. However, when I noticed the queue I completely lost it. As a result of the stuffy air inside the mall and my tardiness, I had given up buying the TV as I had figured it would be pretty hard to carry anyway. I just purchased the PlayStation and left. While waiting in line, I had thought of how isolated I had been from all these things. Indeed, I had not bought anything for myself in ages. I did not follow any popular trends nor moved in parallel with the society for that matter. It felt odd to be facing these facts as I waited in line to pay.

My home felt a lot like me after the PlayStation I purchased. Burak's enthusiasm had intrigued me when he said he had so much fun with his. The TV I bought in one of the tech markets in the center of the city, contributed a lot to the new arrangement of my home. In such a way that I had almost started hearing the click of a Lego piece when I entered each room.

***

On 31 December 2017 midnight, as I gazed up at the sky in San Marco square in Venice, I counted the items I held in my palm one by one. First, my book… Then my home… Last, the job I managed to work at longer than three months… My tax office number… My health insurance… My GP… My red bike… My most precious cat… And certainly, the huge bottle of Prosecco to toast all these…

I was ready now.

Dieci… Nove… Otto… Siete… Sei… Cinque… Quattro… Tre…

Due… Uno…

As I was standing there, under the fireworks, among thousands of people from all around the world, celebrating the finish line of the siege, the bliss I possessed was unfathomably much more beautiful than ever.

CHAPTER II

IMPRESSIONS OF ITALY

LIFE IN ITALY

I managed to fall into the arms of Italy, birthplace of Renaissance. On the surface, my reasons for migrating derived from social reasons aka Turkey. Although, I was undeniably sure from the start, I wanted to live in Italy, not anywhere else. As you've read in the previous chapters, I planned out all my projections about my future accordingly. While nowadays I aim at a simple, uncomplicated life in peace. I can easily confirm that I have accomplished most of these dreams. Nevertheless, nothing is complete yet. Just as in any achievement, persistence is a must here as well.

I am content with what I have so far because big villas, luxurious cars and expensive clothing do not make it to the list of my life standards. I've been good at keeping level with my work schedule. The salary I earn satisfies me. The work-life balance, the room I sleep in, the PC I use, the shoes I wear and many other factors that have an impact on my daily life are fairly good. Whether I add up to these or not is completely up to me. What I mean is if I work harder I'll earn more. Therefore, I'll have more, but in return I will have less time to myself. In the event that the opposite happens, I'll work less, spare more time to myself and subsequently, I'll earn less. That means my travels will become less frequent.

I didn't plan a major shift in my life. It had taken me some time to settle into the current rhythm and I was quite happy about it. My intention was to enjoy what I had at least for the time being. What I meant when I said enjoy was, not a life wrapped around super good quality fun that would be better than the day before.

There are times I battle against the city, its inhabitants, my job. From time to time, I go at war with myself. However, on such occasions, the issue for me is the level of tolerance.

***

If I was asked to summarize my life in Turkey in one word, it would resonate as "unpleasant". I do not know how to express it or where to start, life in Istanbul... To be fair, it is not everyone's experience. After a total of three years in Italy, I have to say I lack a longing for Istanbul. The main reasons are the inappropriate attitude of people I had been with. Plus, the dreadful social system, the horrid streets, the unattractive buildings, the ugly shops and the morality associated with Turkish culture.

I had friends in the beginning who used to tell me off saying "But, Istanbul is a beautiful city!" Some criticized me for leaving. They claim it was a negative reflection of brain drain. Yes, Istanbul is a beautiful city but when one defines a piece of land one should also denote its inhabitants. Air pollution, destruction of green spaces, overpopulation, disrespectful people, traffic problems were factors that rapidly demotivated me. In addition, I found it meaningless to live in an urban area where I had no control over managing my time. On the other hand, I didn't want to be a part of that numb society which easily ignored its recent past. I didn't feel safe in that society who could not raise their voices and go on about their lives as if nothing had happened after seeing an incredibly long list of names on TV. Of people who innocently died, young or old, only because they were present in the wrong place at the wrong time... The society that, over the course of history, deserved virtually nothing because they did nothing.

I very well understood, during my period of seclusion in Bergamo, that the road to chase my dreams would embody to continue believing in my guts rather than accepting defeat to social pressure. Even if the social pressure was created by my own friends.

I was right in ignoring what people had said and done before. After my departure from Turkey, some friends brought me down. It carried me to the verge of depression. There was nothing not to overcome when one blended his schooling with necessary skills. The heart of the matter was to be able to leave one's comfort zone and identify with the character in its essence. The rest seems to follow. It is aboutf being brave.

***

Italy is a country renowned for its utter preservation of its national heritage. It established its population on norms and traditions. In my opinion, it is a patriotic country. They naturally have their political and social problems. Notwithstanding, these are not infiltrated into the individual's daily lives. It is quite difficult to say the high number of African immigrants or their living conditions. The sociological problems between the north and south of the country have traumatic roots. It is reflected on the country's inner dynamic.

Italy does have problems due to its Catholic foundation. Anyhow, I do not want to bore anyone with trivial information. Being a migrant gives me an increased amount of tolerance in everyday life. I hope to give introspect to people who would like to migrate to Italy.

I would like to first introduce the streets. As I have mentioned before, it is quite important for me not to walk on streets that are unattractive. There is distinct harmony almost among all buildings in city centers per se in Italy. All structures, dated or modern, are built both in color and size in harmony with their neighboring others. It holds the form of art dominated by the early days of Christianity. It was composed of ensemble, ratio and order. In those days disharmony meant contortion.

I am horrified by the disharmony of style whenever I intend to compare the cities in Italy architecturally to their substantial equals in Istanbul. Or, other towns in Turkey… When I walk to the center from my flat in Bergamo, I see the building fronts, doors, balconies, shutters and all other details are well placed and beautiful to look at. It truly lifts one's spirits. Just like in the characters in The Sims game when 'environment bar' turns green thanks to pretty frames and decorative items. I, too, breathe an atmosphere of positivity offered by the beauty of these environmental factors. I am in full recognition that Bergamo is a material well-suited for photography. The view behind or the street ahead as I gaze around eating ice cream, ride my bike, observe passersby, their hands full with sketch rolls. I kiss the woman I am with. It is wonderful to acknowledge that no hideous and disproportionate shop signs. Nor are there any discordant structures that bothers me as well-dressed Italians take their dogs for walks.

Certain routines and customs are significant for Italians. They've already had their share of the damage left behind from tourism, which also credited them the benefits. The most recognisable of these is their meal times. They have their breakfast either with a strong coffee or a cappuccino and a croissant; it's a ritual. Chats, greetings, well-wishes while having coffee… They love talking to each other and show their respect by stopping and looking at one another with a "Ciao!" Unlike the majority of people in Turkey, who tend to disrespect each other and hesitate to make eye contact when in the same vehicle, the same waiting room or shopping in the same market. Italians are incomparably respectful.

I can't say it took me a while to get used to closed shutters when it came to lunch time. Shops shut down at midday in order to spare time to socialize and to rest. I learned not to conduct any business at midday in a few months. At lunch time the restaurants are open only a couple of hours and then are closed until dinner. In other words, when the shops close the restaurants open, then the restaurants close and shops open. Therefore, if you want to go to a restaurant in Italy what matters is when the restaurants are open, not when you get hungry. "Aperitivo," a drink with a cost of one drink served together with a few appetizers in cafés or bars before dinner helps you suppress your hunger. It is up to you whether you spend the whole night like this or go to a restaurant after you hang out in these bars a couple of hours. But don't forget, dinner is another ritual for Italians which starts after eight in the evening and continues for at least two hours.

***

Although it differs in each city Italians are generally friendly and kind people. If you speak Italian and manage to tell them what you're after they definitely try to help. It is not at all difficult to make friends or start a conversation wherever you are. However, at this point the ball is in your court. The amount of people who have a good amount of English is very low. So, in the city you live, if you want to make friends or have a circle of friends you have to learn Italian. Otherwise, you will most surely find it troublesome to socialize.

There is a certain degree of conservatism in small or medium-sized towns in Italy, though conservatism seems to be all around the world, no? Italians are bound to their own circles. Most of them act a bit timid to admit newcomers into their network. Though, I believe it has to do more with language than racism. Rule number one: speak their language. If you want to be recognized you must speak their language and respect their culture.

Otherwise, it is impossible for them to trust you. You'd better not let any susceptibility get in the way here because even if it's not in the same degree, as possible in central or northern European countries, in Italy there's still some degree of suspicious approach to aliens. If you reckon they do not trust you and act hostile you'll be at a loss because they are the host here. You have to overcome their suspicion. And the best way to do it is not to take it personally and work yourself up about it when you feel insecure or experience some sort of cynicism. If you want to get yourself accustomed to this notion, it is advisable to remind yourself that the key principle of philosophy of knowledge is method of doubt. If you achieve to stay true to yourself during this period of getting to know one another you will surely be at ease later as Italians are not so guarded. They feel happy when they notice how hard you try to get used to their culture. If you're sympathetic toward foreigners in your country who try to speak your language, and who have learned to cook some basic local food, then you'll know what I mean. Evidently, I cannot speak for the whole of Italy but merely some of the Northern parts I have insight on. Those people are my data.

I got away with both English and a bit of Italian in my process of integration. Since it was not possible for me to make Italian friends who did not speak English, my circle of friends was not so great. Also, those Italian friends who spoke English did not let me know each time they were going out. Either there would be someone who didn't speak English in the group or my friends wouldn't be in the mood to speak English that night.

Some countries do well with English, foreign cultures. Many don't. It is always wise to learn the language of the immigrated country. And in some countries like Italy and even Germany, you have to learn the language. You are allowed to be judgmental about locals' level of English. However, you may not act the same way in their country as it is their own country. There is nothing unnatural about them speaking their mother tongue. Therefore, you should give up saying things like, "Oh these Italians cannot speak English properly. The French don't speak English even if they know it."

***

It is not difficult to get used to Italy in terms of its climate and cuisine as it's not geographically located far from Turkey.

Unlike common knowledge, it is every bit possible to find palatable foods in Italian cuisine other than pasta and pizza. If you're the type of person who cannot easily get used to foreign cuisine and approach it with caution, you still can continue cooking your local dishes in Italy. It is a Mediterranean. The same fruit, vegetables, meat and delicatessen… A bit more pork and variety of wine maybe…

As I lived in northern Italy, springs and autumns were quite wet whereas winters, quite harsh. It is a fact alright that I am no cold weather person but I haven't yet heard anything positive about this region in Italy from Turks. Now we pay the price for those times when we were young and our mothers wrapped us up so tightly in layers. As our bodies show no resistance to cold, in any slight fluctuations in temperature we get cold, and thus, in winter we find ourselves admiring, envying and in awe, staring at Italians who walk in just skirts, long shorts or raincoats.

***

We shouldn't skip the financial aspect of the matter because mountains that you won't be able to climb, delicacies that you won't be able to taste or museums you won't be able to visit will be of no use to you. In order to have access to opportunities this country offers enriched with its history, art, cuisine, nature and many more, one has to have a certain level of income.

Italy's official currency is Euro as it is a part of the eurozone. It is not hard to make a living and pursue a certain life standard in Italy compared to that of Turkey for inflation and euro buying rates are consistent. For example, the price of the ice cream I've been consuming in Italy for the past three years has never changed. The way the coffee I drink is served doesn't reflect any changes in its price. The difference in cost is not three or five Euros but fifty Euro cents, or one Euro max. On the other hand, though the salaries are not high, frugality is present among the Italians just like in their European counterparts. It's not easy to get a bank loan and people do not live in conspicuous consumerism. When considered their active industries in relation to those of Turkey's, they have managed to keep welfare at a level despite current recession. This is proved obvious by the way people dress when they go out to grab breakfast or walk their dogs. Italians, fond of how they look, manage to maintain their standards (good diet, sports, fancy clothes, weekends away in nature) by delaying to upgrade their cars, mobiles phones, laptops or home expenditures.

Italian society in general has understood that gaining life experience and nourishing the soul has much greater significance than purchasing stuff. Thus, their spending habits have been shaped as such. Activities that involve spending time with family and friends, sports outings on weekends, jogging on weekdays, going to concerts, plays and the opera, eating delicious food made with good quality ingredients and drinking good wine are all simple but important details to them.

Similar to every society, it is possible to observe the impacts of American imperialism in Italy. Young generations especially tend to go for the popular and easiest to consume rather than the old and traditional. There is occasional degeneration in terms of music they listen to, the clothes they wear and their nutrition habits, however I can't claim – for now - this is a nationwide phenomenon.

When it comes to life experience, the same generation has the upper hand by traveling, which is an unavoidable fact and they don't refrain from spending money on this. Compiled with inevitable effects of information technologies, the thirst for discovering diverse cultures is on the rise and Italians who have the privilege of holding a passport that is eligible to travel without visas take this opportunity and often go on journeys.

***

As I talked about economics and spending culture above, without having a detour, I would like to touch base on my observations on work ethics and professional habits of Italians.

Italy has not yet caught up with the digital age as strong as other countries did. There is an obvious tardiness in the infrastructure specifically in their telecommunications, media and banking systems. This is related to certain issues in the economy and bureaucracy as well as politics. Certain investments left the country in a certain economic dead-end. Precisely, in a circular economy. This is a result of poor decision making. There exists a properly formed government, bureaucratic regulations that can't be overcome and efforts to equalize the discrepancies between the north and south of the country. Free from bias, I observe that there is a chronic bickering between the north, who accuse the southerners of being lazy, and the south, who accuse the northerners of being ambitious..

When it comes to conducting business both for themselves and for other parties, in my experience, Italians fail to deliver as a result of getting things done at the last minute, mismanaging priorities, time management issues to name but a few. One of my supervisors had told me people in the Lombardy region were hard-working and productive as much as Germans but I disagree. Either I was always located in the wrong region or Italians have different standards.

I should mention the cultural aspect of the issue as well. Italians argue that work/life (life: visits to family and friends, leisure activities, etc.) balance is extremely important. Therefore, they may not want to wear themselves out. Call it old-fashioned, backward or traditionalist; whatever you like… It all results the same and you eventually end up waiting to have your conduct sorted out. That's why, you absolutely have to get into the habit of waiting. During the early days as I was finding it hard to get used to, one of the clerks told me off when I expressed my discomfort, "This is Italy, here nothing is urgent. If you want something done properly you have to wait." I'm in agreement with said about the jobs that involve workmanship. I don't think it justifies tardiness in simple paper work. They are so slow that the most basic data update takes ages.

Once at the airport, the passport police checked my residence permit and asked me about my profession. I replied as bicycle business. He saw the company's name on the screen and asked me to verify it. I nodded and left the checkpoint. I got anxious because the company name he uttered was my first employment place in Italy. I changed three companies until that point.

In short, if you want to do business in Italy and you have to be involved with several channels, I recommend avoiding putting pressure on people. In addition, when you have a business goal in mind, plan ahead knowing people take their time. There's no room to hurry. Italy is one of the top countries in the world with the longest mortality rate.

ABOUT BEING AN EXPAT

In my second year here, I was out drinking with a young group of people including a few Turkish citizens. They, as well, were expats. I witnessed their list of complaints about Italy. Whether they worked in Bergamo or were students at the time, each complained about something else, making comparisons to their previous host cities. I couldn't make any sense as to their complaints as they, again, had previously been nagging about those cities as well in no time at all. I reckon, two of the basic characteristics of human nature are sociability and adaptability, in general, compliance to what necessitates in current situations. Some people are unable to transform such components together with wit into convenience. I believe they have problems with their own points of view, rather than the place they reside in.

Attempts to be made once you step foot in a new town, be it long or short-term, as an immigrant are more or less clear... You learn the language, discover social opportunities and benefit from them. You get used to dining and wine drinking culture. While you're at it, you make friends so that this will help take the edge off the difficulties of the first steps. It would be great if one could make acquaintance of other immigrants who have been through the same process. This might mean the days spent alone would be less intense but safer with company.

The only issue that might negatively impact one is the dismay of changing, even fragmenting identity. I understand that it is reasonable to leave the past behind; but, when not processed properly, people tend to stay on their own.

The result of an emotionally unprocessed immigration can be difficult. One can neither properly exist in their host country nor their homeland. This limbo pushes them toward ultimate loneliness, unsociability, reluctance in having fun and consequently, departing from that place.

***

Failure of integration is a phenomenon I have observed especially during the first stages of immigration. Despite all those years that passed, I know of people who still eat only the food of their country of origin and buy their groceries accordingly. Preserving the old against the new, not giving up on what you're used to, suspicion mixed with fear, shyness, lack of confidence etc. can all be overcome. It is about attitude.

In my opinion one of the major problems of individuals brought up in today's world is attending to personal growth unseemingly. Generations who seek concepts such as learning and self-development only at schools, in course books, academic articles, newspaper clippings by their favorite columnists and in self-help books by newbies who boast about listing their own achievements, do get estranged from themselves as a result. Also, those books have no use when confronted with real hardship or conflict, in life.

This generation who have accomplished all knowledge and experience by their mid-twenties only methodologically, stand at a distance against any obstacle. From time to time, this distance leads to anxiety and whatever is new – person, place, event or situation – is ignored altogether. On the contrary, learning never ceases. It just shapeshifts and continues in an uncommon way.

I think there is a correlation between self-development and attitude toward new situations. During one of his speeches, Steve Jobs talks about connecting the dots. People who are accomplished, have resemblances amongst their stories. They influence many. Authors, business people, artists… In those stories, educational backgrounds are proven to be overrated. It possibly offers different points of view in making sense of the world. Yet it does not offer short-cuts in life. People have to draw their own frames, their paths.

Skills, things enjoyed during childhood, childhood dreams, education, social connections, life experience and some courage make up the milestones of a character. I don't think these are independent entities. Family training, schooling, social skills revealed in childhood while they constitute many things, they do not define or justify actions.

***

People long for their homelands from time to time. It is normal. The danger is to create a never passing sense of nostalgia. Living in the past..

Nobody snatches childhood memories from anyone. Nor are they erased. Constantly making them priority ruins the moment. At this instance it is important to put fear and longing aside. It is essential to turn the focus on how to engage with the new environment in a peace of mind.

Even though it is a planned step for the purposes of work or education, the concept and moving away are only the tip of the iceberg. The long emotional process of migrating or integrating, with its phases, is a whole other thing than the leaving itself. In my opinion, the first reactions to living abroad, more or less, define the type of immigrant experience or attitude you adopt in the new country.

It is impossible to stay unaffected within a flowing and inconsistent world. The major issue here is how to reflect that change and rate of the skills to be utilized.

What the city you left behind used to offer you or its activities may not be the same as the new city's offerings. This doesn't mean there is nothing to do in the new environment. It is pretty difficult to show people who are stuck in their own perspective that there is also allure around the new kingdom. People can reinstate new pleasures in place of old habits. However, explaining that can become time-consuming and exhausting. In such circumstances, I always urge those people to try to reach out to their true selves. By that, I mean for the persons to remember the attributes about themselves, have them list all the things they enjoy. Then slowly they realize how much they're actually capable of and contradict with themselves for a second.

Our hobbies or the way we enjoy life is sometimes shaped by our own choices. Other times, by the amenities our city offers. If you want to use a mountain bike in a concrete jungle you have to have a car to carry it until there. You can drive to the woods or hills and then ride your mountain bike. If you don't have a car but still would like to ride a mountain bike, you have to get a road bike, so you can ride on asphalt. This way, you may leave your abode and ride your bike on a nearby, most suitable street.

I believe observing nature helps to leave the past thoughts aside for a while. Nature is not part of a temporary existence. What are the most popular activities in that city? Is there a lake? Is the ocean close by? Are the woods, hills or rivers within reach? What kind of alternatives are there? How is transportation provided? How do people spend their long-term holidays? Finding answers to these is more useful than reminiscing about past habits.

Searching for what else is a constructive approach towards building a relationship with the present. After all, the residents of this city as well need to relieve stress, cherish their love for nature and touch the earth or the water together with their families, don't they? Right at this point something that doesn't appear in the books come in handy: the skill of adaptability. In order to continue the immigration process properly adaptability is a must. This is possible through having an open mind. You can either grow your social circles by acquiring new experiences. Or, you keep on complaining and count down until you get back to your pre-immigrant status.

There is a huge difference between going to a place knowing you'll be back and going to a place for relocation. This difference affects everything that will have an impact on you starting from your supermarket shopping to purchasing your bed.

***

Perhaps I sound like I am preaching but I would like you to know that what I share here is solely based on my own experiences and observations. At the end of the day, it is completely your decision to determine how to respond to whom and where. Locating a group of people from your homeland and pursuing their footsteps is also an alternative but I didn't choose that way. I prefer to meet every challenge myself. Otherwise, you could, of course, become a member of that group through social media and meet lots of expats. Maybe, possibly minimize your loneliness. It is important to know that when you don't choose this path, loneliness is not the only disadvantage.

You should leave all prejudice behind when you befriend people without knowing their individual social and cultural background. In short, you shouldn't take everything for granted and assume what they say or do are correct just because they are Westerners. How many of those people who keep saying, "Europe is way ahead of your country! They've got this!" have actually lived in Europe? Visiting a place and living in that place are two separate things. Yes, certainly they are ahead of the few countries in many aspects but in which regards? Or which part of those countries? If you've invested in yourself, can speak at least one foreign language fluently and internalised critical thinking, you will not face any obstacles in distinguishing one person from another. Getting to know a culture and representatives of that culture thoroughly is avoiding prejudice and having open communication.

***

Stepping into becoming an immigrant is like choosing your level when you start a new computer game. It's multi-layered and has too many variants. It has different benefits or disadvantages depending on if you're alone or with your spouse or with your family. I arrived here alone so my trials were mainly spiritual. Actually, no one dies but all of a sudden you are left alone as if they had all passed away. Just as in having nobody to cling to when you receive bad news, you don't have anybody to share good news, either. And you always have to take good care of yourself because you know when you get sick there won't be a family member sitting by your side or a pal you can call and ask to come over. These things inevitably help you mature. But I also must add that the maturity and experience you acquire instill in you a terrific self-confidence. Once you've started achieving things that you never thought you could and understood what you're capable of, you're so much more motivated for the next round. You've finally arrived and your head is high up this time.

EPILOGUE

It is impossible to figure out everything that might happen when you move abroad. Just like many decisions you've made and will make, becoming an immigrant might bring in unpredictable results. Maybe it will cast you into an unfathomable corner in your life. You can be as mindful you are, people are random. You can't have control over the people you interact with, or their lives. Even over what those lives might throw at you, for that matter. Thus, within the flow of all these, do not let the mistakes you occasionally make bring you down. Try to remember, you are in control of your own life each moment you don't feel strong enough. You will be the sole instigator of whatever happens to you, be it good or foul. If you're ready for this inkling and if you're thrilled by it, you are ready to move as well.

Remember the time, when you hit your head as a child and your parents pretended they were mad at the object you'd hit your head on.. a make-believe to take away your pain... As an adult, make-believe is no longer an option. You need to take full responsibility for your actions. Otherwise, you will never actually exist in the land you will get to call "home" or in any other country you may land.

To conclude, don't forget, you're the new kid in town. If you want to make people warm up to you, love you and accept you, you should be willing to share your toy cars, your teddy bears, dolls and your most precious Lego parts with them...

CHAPTER III

DIARY

21 November 2016

There are two tyres laid by my bedside. Their both sides are yellow and they smell divine. No, they haven't been used yet and it appears they will not be for a while. Nowadays, the weather is constantly foggy and rainy.

They are bike tyres… The tyres that belong to the bike which has brought me here… No, no; I didn't come here on a bike. They are just the tyres of my precious white bicycle and are waiting for their turn to give me a ride on a dry day.

Not a day goes by without clouds gathering up in the sky in this city. Sometimes they're so high up and we still get wet. And other times, they come down right next to us because they wonder how we all have been. I know; you are going to ask me if this is enough to gratify them. I don't assume so since they come so close that we hardly see anything else. The other side of the street, the building across the street, the car approaching and many more…I believe they act a bit ungenerously.

***

I didn't come here on a bike. It was a lie. I actually came here with a bike; I just wasn't on it. I was with it, next to it. And it was next to me.

We had met a few years ago. I was lost, didn't know what I wanted. I just needed a change.

For a lengthy period, the idea of a change occupied my mind every day. I rode my bike to different lands in foreign countries, to other towns, streets and I rode it to get to other people. I thought I would find what I was looking for in its company. I believed, if I got close enough, I could be near enough. There were times I was so close to what I was looking for; I felt it in my bones but I also knew there were others to get to. When I arrived at one I kept missing the other; and when I approached the other, there was another one that I had missed.

"More," I would say, "there is more than this."

My pace was fine. I was seeing all that I wanted to see, climbing all the hills I wanted to prevail. It was magnificent to gaze over the earth from up above.

There should have been no finality to the hills I wanted to pace. When I reached one I should be able to observe the next one, I ought to have found the path to take me there. If I were tired I would search for a shortcut; but, if I were not, then I most certainly must go up that hill.

One day everything turned out to be indiscernible from one of those hills. That hill was obviously higher than the one before. It certainly was not the highest on earth. I didn't know what was blocking my view. There were no clouds. Neither up over the sky nor around me... I couldn't figure it out.

Were there no hills left to climb?

Not possible.

I'm still on the same hill. How am I supposed to stay here? What if other hills are prettier? The ones I've climbed so far were all so beautiful until I climbed them; and yet, the next might be even prettier.

The world is so immense and gorgeous... How can one not get flustered over the time wasted amidst all this uncertainty and diverseness? I confess...

I, in fact, had this hill on my mind a long time ago. It was so magnificent... On a clear sky I sometimes was able to see its summit from far away. I had been to many other hills, gone up to summits. I did remember how they all made me feel. It was exactly for this reason I so much wanted to be here.

At first, I didn't know how to get there. I asked around. Many didn't know, either. Those who knew hadn't been themselves, they had heard of it from others. I read, searched, learned, faltered, learned again, faltered again. Nothing worked.

I could have reached there if I wanted to... But how, with what?

Bicycles were my ultimate chariot.

Nobody had thought of that.

3 December 2016

It's Saturday. I quit work on Tuesday. Either I quit or they let me go. Both are possible.

Christmas is three weeks from now. I see Christmas trees everywhere that cats would love to go up and bring down. All lit, decorated, colorful and huge…

***

Last year I, too, had a Christmas tree. A tree Niccolò and Siena had played with and torn off all its decorations…

Now, here, I could have bought a new tree but I don't have money for it. Neither do I have my cats with me. Just like many other things in my life they stayed behind. Somewhere in the past. I don't feel their presence at home. Who knows, at which sharp hairpin turn they disappeared…

***

Why am I going through this severe testing? There's got to be a reason for everything ultimately hitting rock bottom when they were initially going alright…

I carried my life away. I brought everything here; spare parts, my clothes, shoes, towels, medicine et al.. I took them by the hand and brought them here with me. I had a talk with them one by one. I said, "Look! This is your new home." Of course, at first they found it odd. Some of them didn't like their closet, some, the lighting in their spot…Some said, "We can't survive without hangers," but they, too, got used to staying folded up.

They were cross with me because I left them too long in the house by themselves. "We can't even get to see your face, what's the meaning of living here then?" they kept saying.

"Why isn't the weekend enough for you?" I asked. They were hurt.

And then the weather turned sour.

***

But now we have plenty of time together. I pay special attention to avoid communicating with my trousers and shirts. They need time alone. But I try to attend to the rest. They're angry. And they're right because I neglected them. I am trying to make up to them nowadays, though this time, they really are anxious. They don't need to express it, I can tell by looking at them. There's doubt oozing from their eyes…

They look like they wouldn't want to move again. It is so obvious they are exhausted…

"It didn't work!" I say… "What could I do? Do you have any idea what I've gone through in order to bring you here? Do you know how much stuff I had to let go? Are you aware of how much money I spent?

They sulked when they heard me raise my voice. They pursued their lips, turned around and walked away.

I said "No!" to so many things to come here…

I didn't ask for things to happen this way… There were no obstructions on my journey here. Alas, how could I predict what's at the end of the road? There were twists and bumps but the motorway was always neat… I believed it would continue like that so I drove on ignoring the signs.

Then everything happened all of a sudden. I found myself at a roadblock made by pebbles, soil and that giant felled tree. What's more, this time it wasn't my cats who flipped the tree over. I looked around to see who was responsible for it, but couldn't see anybody.

I can't go back now.

6 December 2016

I'm sitting in the kitchen on one of the couches eyeing around effortlessly. I didn't take off my dark brown shoes; my feet are up on the kitchen table.

My eyes are dried up and I'm finding it hard to move.

The weather is awesome. Not a cloud in sight and the temperature has reached double digits for the first time in a long while. The sun's reflection from the building across bothers me but I'm too lazy to move. I'm extremely comfy right now.

***

Everything seems frozen. I have to buy groceries, I want to eat something and I want to go out in the sun but I feel so beat as if I had consumed all my energy on getting dressed and now I have no fuel left to go out…

I have to find my eyedrops. I could feel each time my eyelids move. They're heavy and my eyes sting because they're so dry.

Floors are filthy, I haven't done the washing-up. Never have I lasted this long without cleaning my bike.

I want to do something but then I make up excuses in my mind so I don't do them.

Well, the sun is set as I think of all those. There's no need to walk fast from the shade.

I clench my teeth a lot. They will erode. If I keep to the same pace they will be their half size soon. Stress is such a foe…

When there is no hope there is nothing.

I'm so tired. So beaten.

Not one soul I love is here with me. I am in no condition to do anything I love doing. For some of the things I want to do there isn't enough people around, and for others, certain conditions are not matched.

I hate riding my bike in the cold. It's such a drag to put the right gear on, let alone taking them off …

I memorized the timing of the church bells.

It's time to go to my unmade bed in my pants and jumper and sleep.

8 December 2016

Here I am again; in the kitchen, sitting by the oven right next to the counter. My coffee should be ready soon. I will again spill some of it while I pour, and again, I'll feel too lazy to wipe it.

It's pretty awkward to live in a kitchen where there is no cooking. So is getting up off my bed in the middle of the night just to go lie down on another bed.

I have a couple of single couches in red covering. They both are against the windows. They're very comfortable but I usually sit on the one that faces the door sideways. The carpet in the kitchen is not long enough to reach as far as the other couch. I hate wearing slippers or walking in socks around the house. The flooring is not wood but a marble patterned vinyl with a total of eight triangles of three different colors in each square. I don't know about the rest of the house. If I'm correct, there are 520 of these squares in the kitchen and each one is colder than the other.

The chair I'm now sitting on, goes with the table which I centered in the kitchen. I write on this table. It has cigarette burns on its surface. It's enough to look up at the ceiling to have an idea that the tenants before were smokers. The connecting corners have all turned yellow because of smoke. There stands a beautiful fireplace in the opposite corners. Its chimney has been removed. When I first found out about it I was pretty upset but I'm used to it now. In order not to feel unhappy each time I take a look, I rested my bike against the front of it. From then on, all I see when I look in that direction is my bike. Fireplace doesn't even cross my mind.

Yes, we could have had cherishable memories. The sounds that small wood makes could have given a totally different feeling to me, and its odor, a totally different atmosphere to the house. Perhaps I would have cooked something. My coffee wouldn't have gone cold too quickly, I would have terribly enjoyed it each time I sipped coffee from my mug.

I love the coffee in Italy but, with the fireplace here, I could have known how Turkish coffee made on wood fire tasted.

On days I had gone out without my gloves on, I would come back home and approach the fireplace. I tried to rewarm my very cold hands after rubbing them together, and kept them there until I felt they'd burn. I would drink mulled wine. I would probably have sat cross legged on a plush carpet I'd placed right in front of it, let my face warm up, feel drowsy and then curl up there and sleep. I thought about the women I had loved. Or those who had loved me…Perhaps my love would have been next to me. I would have moved a bit to make space for her. Maybe my cat could have been with me and as he curiously bent over the fire he'd have his whiskers burned and would never go near a fire again. Perhaps I would have purchased a rocking chair in the darkest tone of brown and spent every waking hour on it. I would have placed everything I ever would be needing under my nose and so I could reach out and grab my magazines, books and wine-stained notebook.

But, like I said, these don't even cross my mind anymore.

I have a bike.

18 December 2016

I moved into my new house, made arrangements. Things didn't stay in order for long. A few tables moved around and a couche got sent to another room.

Some furniture had chunks of dust underneath. I guess they had never been shifted.

I brought the desk to my bedroom as I planned to write there.

I've now realized it has been exactly two months since I moved in here. Not once did I sit at this desk within those two months to do writing properly.

***

I feel so rootless. I am detached from where I have grown up in. It's like I don't have any people of my own…I have no friends who know my childhood, with whom I grew up and played together, whom I told about my first girlfriend…

I don't see anyone from my childhood days, primary or high school… They have got lost in time.

None left who knows me inside out.

It is not that I never saw it coming. It was actually me who pushed myself to solitude. There were moments when I wanted to go back but things never worked out the way I wanted. I couldn't have faith, I was never reassuring. I couldn't love, wasn't able to make anyone loved. It just didn't happen. It was either the words someone iterated, or in the minds of some others'… I undermined the limits of imagination of some, and the ideologies of some others'…

I am the he-who-knows-it-all.

Never in my life were things centered. Never my money, nor my career, nor my family, nor my friends… Somehow, I was never able to center them. I got close only once, but hey, I then stumbled upon a stupid boss. The rest was a succession of events.

I wonder if it's me who likes to destroy? I do not know what it is that I don't see.

Do I so much like constant shifting? Or am I frightened of putting down my roots? Well, having a few buddies, a few childhood friends doesn't necessarily mean having your own roots…

I don't even let my belongings be. I destroy their harmony as well. I'm thinking, what if they stayed where they were, what would have changed in my life?…

I can't find the answer to that.

5 January 2017

I don't have any wine left. I don't have a spoon with a long enough handle to dig deep into the coffee jar either. This stench is probably coming from the dirty dishes and the garbage I haven't chucked in two complete weeks. Carpet looks faded. Must be because I have been walking about the flat in my shoes. Cigarette burns on couch covers, the grey dust on the table and my hair particles gradually increasing in the sink…

None of that matters because I don't have a bike anymore.

***

They stole my bike last night.

They stole my beautiful bike; its blue looked so pretty from behind, the one that I picked for my love of nature, as it is my refuge; the yellow of it I admired so much.

They stole my bike, which I never got tired of cleaning after each ride, made it look as if it were brand new; its pedals and handlebars all white.

They stole my bike, my precious bike which I placed in the most sanctuous corner of my home. The one I even washed in the bath when it was filthy, my darling bike which I took wherever I went.

They stole my bike, which pet me on my back as I was leaving my homeland with a shattered heart and broken promises.

They stole my bike, which I traveled to countless cities and countries with, which I touched so many lives together with, had memories with and mattered together; my white bike…

They stole my bike, the bike which stood next to me when passers by stopped and admired my bike as I sat at the top of Selvino and looked down at the village.

They stole my bike; my precious bike which I checked first if it was ok even before I checked my bleeding knee after a steep fall in Medun in the storm.

They stole my bike, which the cars cheered with honking horns on a climb to Feldberg after crossing the Swiss-German border.

They stole my bike, which couldn't keep still when it saw me after a flight even if it was cold and pressed but looking all lively between all those suitcases.

They stole my bike, which heard me swear riding on never-ending hills, wasn't bothered about my dripping sweat, stood mighty and composed after my full pull of exertion.

They stole my bike, which was adamant to take a break at the most stunning views, the one which shook by a strong wind, then was relieved to have been rested on its least two parts.

They stole my bike, which I rode to the city center in my jeans and placed right across from myself on a busy street as I sipped my coffee in a café.

They stole my bike, which I willingly lent my friends to for test drives who were curious about it.

They stole my bike, which got tedious at the service stations afraid they would leave a stain on it, got cross if the gears were not fixed properly.

They stole my bike which, while riding I was all sweats, tired, singing, talking on the phone, watching the sky, missing my mates, dreaming of my cats, desiring the woman I loved next to me and imagined many more dreams to come true.

Not only did they steal my bike; they also kidnapped countless hopes I held on to.

15 June 2017

Struggles for the new job, the move, new people, new smell... Now I'm back at the same spot...

I was an inhabitant in another city for three months. I observed the world from the surrounding mountains. I photographed that town's people, tried the drinks there, laughed at the jokes, and as if I was not astounded by all that, I left that city in a heartbeat.

I spent half the days of every spring month in a darkest house, doing a job which at first excited and then bored me to death as usual, my weight fixed at 65 kilos.

Just like all others before, I was not to blame. I had tried a family company this time not considering the fact that I performed well in regular companies I had worked at.

Well, so be it. Experience is what counts.

***

Small towns in Veneto resemble charismatic women who make you fall in love with them by their ability to talk and influence. I can't call them beautiful or sexy because I am unable to look at pretty faces of women. I am interested in the curves or the elegance of their wrists and ankles of women.

Cute women's hair smells delicious and the colors of their sloppy but well-paired clothes are always vivid. Some pretend to be shy despite being the opposite and play hard to get. It proves quite skillful. They handle this so well that I act resigned to it and become part of the game, not letting it get ruined. Then, I start to like it, I get used to it. I play the game.

***

The thing I get sick of most in those towns is when they welcome rainy days one after the other. I clean the shades of grey the town left on me, rub them off my shoes, my cuffs and want to continue my life as if nothing had happened. But, no! Days are so long, clouds are so identical that it becomes routine now. Weather websites continually show rain in their ten-day forecasts. Whereas, I dislike routine and stay away from anything that is predicted or planned ahead.

I am not exactly sure if it's because of relentless rain or ceaseless curiosity, the glasses I possess do not take long to be filled up. And, when they're full I leave the current location, leave them, without ever breaking or spilling them.

I used to care about other people's opinion about me. I left too many people, places or things behind… It no longer makes sense. I am used to deserting those half-expressed opinions, which get lesser as I get older…

17 June 2017

Why don't you buy new ones in place of those glasses… They're neither deep enough nor clean enough… You've rubbed them, cleaned them using everything you could find but some of the stains won't come off.

You'd better take good care of the place you live in… You should drink delicious wine in beautiful tumblers. Whether you're by yourself or not, do the things you do nicely and well, then you'll certainly have pleasure.

Try to enjoy things. Drink the coffee you prefer, eat what you really like… Even if you unhappily consume it, eat it… Even if you couldn't manage to take good care of your soul, you have to take care of your body.

Leave the dripping taps, buzzing light bulbs or loud clocks be… Don't mind them. Don't think!

Don't mind the noise motorbikes make on the street, either. However much high-pitched it is, never mind. Also, you've asked for all this. I mean, it was your choice to live in the city center. They're cities after all, no matter how small they are, nobody could easily quit city centers.

Today is your mother's birthday. Have you told her your good wishes? Your eyes are closing, I know. But, you weren't like this a little while ago. You were checking air tickets again, you can't fool me… Are you sulking because you couldn't go to the place you wanted to go?

Hang up that phone! I'm asking for your attention!

This can't be the house of your dreams. There are just too many objects that belong to others in this house. Too much dust, filth, happenings and neglect… This is not you. Neither is this life.

You are an utterly different person.

19 June 2017

Desire and courage to write dawns on me after a few beers. I am in a bar near one of the parks in the city where birds can be heard. There are a lot of wooden chairs. Feels like it opened just for the sake of it. I like Lambic beers a lot; but if I continue at this speed I will regain all the weight I lost.

I can't sit still. I can't seem to live without anxiety. I can't figure out when and where my constantly delayed anxieties will show their faces; but I do hope they don't strangle me in my most vulnerable time such as now.

I feel unable to stay put in the cities I visit. I guess I was one of the few who got bored in Amsterdam before 48 hours were up. Or here, in Berlin, who started looking for another place to visit just because I stayed on for more than a day… But, I'm not the only one to blame. This city has no tone. What I mean is there isn't anything that calls for you in the streets. It is a city built from scratch but its dwellers were not really considered obviously. They have focused more on the people in the cars. Everything and everywhere is big and wide. Bikes are also an item in all this spaciousness but it is not glamorous.

***

If I am to categorize people as those whose spirits rise when they drink and those that don't, I believe I would be in the same category with those who just drip down a glass. I want to go to Prague from here but I have no energy. And I'm pretty sure it is not as a result of physical exhaustion. I want to go back to my condo in Bergamo and sleep for hours.

Where I'm sitting now is warm but I feel an occasional breeze. It's just about enough to cool my forehead and hair roots if I pull my head up. This bar is called Macke Prinz. I've just noticed. They play moody tracks. The bartender is quite fun and pleasant. He looks as if he had been placed there to neutralize the atmosphere.

In fact I came here to meet a young Italian woman whom I have been in contact with on Instagram in the past years. Her name is Gloria. I wanted to meet her because her story is very similar to mine. Just like me, she ran away from her own country to find a better vision in another. I ran from Turkey to Italy whereas she moved from Italy to Germany. What could be the life lesson here? To be honest, I don't know either. I'll ask her.

***

There are cities that are photography material. Cities who's windows, doors and streets you fall in love with...

None of the German cities I visited so far were like this. It seems being a developed country didn't bring with itself attractions to watch. In short, German cities stand separate when it comes to looking over a city at sunset somewhere from the top… There is utmost respect for people on bikes but this is not sufficient… I didn't see any old guys here who rode their bikes without helmets, for example. Those types, who show off on their chic bikes, tanned and wear their hair combed back, do provide some character to such places channelling their souls. People who startle you and generate some sort of laughter in you when you look at them, the type of people you won't forget wherever you go, people who deserve respect… An opportunity rises to broaden horizons during a coffee chat with these people who have become that city's or region's milestones.

I finished my beer. I don't want to spend a lot. There's just so much I can do on my own. How much can I drink after all? Or how much can I travel without getting tired? How many streets can a day hold? In how many parks can I search for a bench in the shade?

And they all have a bottleneck. Rather tight on me, not so well fitted on me as I imagined…

***

You know how people call those who are unable to hold a job or get into a routine: "they can't settle down…" What exactly is settling down? What do we do to be defined to have settled down? Would I have started to settle down, for example, if I had gone for a drink with a couple of friends after work like the guy in khakis and an incredibly mismatched belt and blue shirt sitting cross from me now? Or is pursuing such a life a sign of setting down? It is presumed that routine and peace and consistency are organically linked, but I doubt that.

I'm not attacking the people who like to lead a life such as that. If it is what makes them happy then nobody has the right to judge them. However, I do believe the number of people who are happy this way or who find it easy to adapt to are decreasing everyday. In short, the number of people who are aware of what they have gotten themselves into is increasing. This is more of an observation than an opinion. I hear it, I see it… What is shared on social media, constant grouching in Whatsapp groups, articles regarding alternative stories of fleeing sent around family members in the hope that what is written might be of interest to their offspring, and many more of these examples reveal that humanity is awakening. Even if its speed is somewhat slow, enlightenment is what it is: enlightenment. What matters most here is not its speed but where it's headed and its point of arrival. All I'm wondering is what exactly has started to make way for minds…

Lack of time?

Or lack of love?

22 June 2017

I ended up in Amsterdam, Berlin and, eventually, Prague, even though I was leaving home to go for a swim. I said goodbye to these cities that welcomed me for 5-6 days and now I'm on my way to Bergamo from Prague, sitting in a tiny seat, my knees and legs joined together.

I took a nap. Afterwards, I couldn't get away from the announcements or the air-stewardesses trying to sell some things… I eyed the view out of the window next to seat 9A for a long time. We're flying over the still-snow-covered Alps, now, in June, which I climbed just a few days back. They look magnificent, and also give the impression that they're here to remind us of something. Each time I go up high and disengage from people, my faith in sustaining a life without them comes in parallel to my inner piece.

***

Yesterday I visited Franz Kafka Museum in Prague. I read all I could there. How fortunate he was to have lived through the years of World War I and witness it. Or perhaps.. we should say, unfortunate… When you think of Milena dying in a concentration camp, still so much in love with him, it's unfortunate. But, if you think of how this all contributed to his art, it is lucky. And it is our luck to be able to have access to his writing because they came this far. His private life, his women, family, his disagreements with his father… I read many very familiar lines. The letter he had written to his father was preserved as it was. "Everything you said is correct, all else is in absolute wrong, unacceptable and ludicrous," it says.

I would have loved to listen to him during his era, look closely into his dilemmas.

23 June 2017

Solitude is the most wonderful thing. You take on nobody's responsibility. You aren't accountable for anything. You don't have to wait up or ask anyone to do so. Although it brings more loneliness I do not have anything but solitude these days…

I want to get rid of the people around me if they should attempt to make me go through something that will bother me. I do not question whether this is a healthy, normal or harmful thing. Still, you know the pleasure you sometimes feel when you're alone and the unique luxury to keep silent when you want to, I wouldn't change it for the world. When people tell me things, even for my own sake, I feel they interfere with my life. Then, I transform into a cat whose fur stands up along its spine because I feel threatened. I am filled with hatred and I turn into a man grinding his teeth.

I panic when I place people in the center of my life. People who I knew nothing about for 20-25 years, I didn't grow up with, and when I talk to them a lot and become good friends. I know they will do something that will trouble me and I will not want them to be around anymore. And it is what happens eventually. I put a lot of pressure on myself to socialize but I really can't tolerate much after a certain point. I just want to have a good time. And, maybe, to find the love of my life… To chase after that person and observe the world together. I want lives that are presented in the fairy tales. That they call the fairest skin of all, which smells divine…

***

As I wake up to neck aches, a good sleep won't even help sometimes. I can't wake up feeling alright and it gets hard to fall asleep in the night.

I close my eyes.

The wind forces the shutters to open and they close again roughly making noise. I get up to stabilize them. Soon as I close my eyes I start to hear the empty bottle sounds made in the bins - it's trash collection day - and glasses are the priority in the recycling process. I don't know how many times the truck makes rounds during the day but definitely more than once because I am pretty sure I have woken twice by the same noise. When the truck's work is done the nearby church bells start their shift to keep me awake. And it's quite long… I even memorized their tune.

I get into a different position in bed and face another wall to watch. The first thing people do when they come home from work is to walk their dogs. And the first thing dogs do is to bark when they spot one another or feel threatened.

I can't blame the number of coffees I consume during the day because I pedal and climb like crazy so I should be dead beat.

The weather is so hot and stuffy and I sweat a lot in bed. My pillow is soaked. Motorbikes add up to this tasteless meal, too…These cheap motorbikes that produce horrific sounds out of their engines have the same effect on me as in the days when I used to commute by bus, and while trying to sleep, I would get woken up by a miserable move the bus would make getting into pits. As my head dropped, I'd suddenly open my eyes and get used to all the ugliness that I didn't want to see over again.

My joints ache because of insomnia. I'm tired.

I am more angry, tired and unhappy than the woman who swears and pulls on the horn when she sees there's another car parked at the entrance of her own garage.

***

My loneliness never ever subsides.

I'm trying to make up situations where this is a normal welcome in order to stay sane because I don't want my mind to focus on the fact that this actually is pretty weird.

I wanted to go to the beach by myself and swim along. But then, going to the beach alone sounded very pathetic. It doesn't make sense to swim away from the shore by myself. Moreover, I could go ahead and attempt to not have come back. Therefore, I had a complete change of plan and went to Amsterdam with a backpack. Off to Berlin after that, and then, to Prague… I only stayed a couple of nights most in these cities and I didn't understand why I was there in the first place.

The night before I left Bergamo, I found out it was a movie and concert night. Yet, everything was in Italian and I didn't understand it. You have to be a native where you live... It felt so bland to be involved in these activities on my own and I was so unhappy I wanted to leave the city. If I were not there, neither would be the activities. If I didn't hear music then there was no music. Knowing people are having fun out there while I was home got on my nerves. Thus, I left them be with what belonged to them.

But when I returned I felt like I was home. On top of that, more than how I had felt in the city I was born.

24 June 2017

I'm about to start the loneliest dinner ever. I have come to my favorite restaurant. Ordered the most delicious dishes. It's actually pretty hard to find anything that is not tasty in Italian cuisine. You should either go to a place off the beaten track or pop into one of those touristic joints for that. Otherwise, it's nearly impossible.

They'll be serving my favorite dish on the menu very soon but I don't know how it will taste while I'm all alone. There's nobody to make a toast with. But, hey, there's a wonderful Prosecco from Valdobbiadene on the table.

I'm drinking by myself; I have to. My order is about to be served. By my order, I don't mean a big meal. A mixed salad and pasta with a delicious sauce... I am on the enclosed portion of the patio overlooking the street which is open and airy in summer; and no matter what I order there are always flies in the bread basket. These useless houseflies are regular customers of each table... I say useless because I don't know their function. I know the function of everything I've ever encountered so far in my life. It's only these flies that I don't know the function of.

Maybe they also think I'm useless. Really, what use am I?

***

I am the clientele the restaurants like most. Since I was a child I didn't like sitting at a table for long. In fact, I can't. As soon as I finish my course I start fidgeting, I constantly change my position, fiddle with cutlery and start looking around.

Quick rounds are vital for restaurants with plenty of customers. They really like me here because I don't overstay at the table. From time to time they even host me at a reserved table. They're amenable as they're aware I'll only stay for half an hour. On the plus side, I'm no hassle. For example, I asked for a beer but they brought Prosecco.

Sometimes I let myself go with the flow, it's better. Should I have returned it and asked for my beer instead? When you're alone, these types of things are manageable. Now, if I had somebody sitting across from me she could have opted out of Prosecco and ordered another drink. Way too much hassle… Summon the waiter, explain the situation, return the drink, wait for the new drink to arrive… I have already finished my course and drink as I am telling you this. A light dessert, a strong coffee and we're good to go! Finished.

I check the time, not even an hour since I arrived and I clearly finished a meal under a time limit usually allocated for two persons. Besides, I was writing. It means there are actually two people at this table. One is myself, and the other is, again, myself. My handwriting was off for a bit while eating. Well, so be it…

***

I'm sweaty. It's nearly eight p.m. but it's still very hot in the city. The sun is about to set but it's sweltering. I keep my shirt collars open for some air as I walk about the town. I need to keep my heart cool.

***

I have come to the spot where I sat after a bike ride when I used to live in Dalmine; I hadn't yet moved to this street. I frequent this place: Bar La Funicolare. Each time they see me they greet me and ask about my book, my bike and Turkey.

Cars drive by. Bikes pass by. I have another sip of my drink and enjoy doing absolutely nothing. Pretend as if there's no tomorrow…

My mind has now started affirmations… When I say affirmations, I actually feel like they are a necessity… Especially while writing… Thoughts that have never yet occurred to me now appear to have comfortably lodged themselves in my sitting room. Nor touching the sides of the couch with their sticky fingers as those irritating guests do… Things get more sticky, they stick to you more.

All the ugliness in the world feels unendurably offensive now with all my wit. Yes, I can't tolerate it, I also want to fight it. I guess, for this also, I have to feel present. A messy contradiction…

This bar is called La Funicolare because it is located right next to the cable car that goes up to the old town and people can purchase their tickets from here when the kiosk is closed. I could buy a very cheap ticket and go up there in thirty seconds or follow the steps up and be there in less than ten minutes. Lots of beautifully-dressed women scrutinize one another in a two-cabin sized carriage. They like the idea of arriving at their destination quickly because their heels would not last those historical steps.

***

My eyes rest on women in sundresses with strikingly matching boots crossing the street right ahead. Some have an obvious look of athletic background. Their leg muscles are so distinct like in the countries in the Africa continent with meticulously defined borders. You wouldn't notice such aesthetic details if you don't care about anything in the world. I guess, I still do…

***

Anxiety…

I bite my nails. Also inside my cheeks and lips.

I'm trying to forgive the people I ditched and look for excuses to reconnect with them but I can't. I just can't. In fact, sometimes I feel quite courageous and it kind of looks like I'm getting there, then, knowing the person to be forgiven is going to get cheeky and judgmental with me and I momentarily give up.

I can take care of my own welfare, just, I won't have anyone to tell me what to do, that's all. Getting judgmental is another issue. People love to judge others by reflecting upon results of all their traumas. Mostly, due to the mistakes they've made or that they fear to make.

I do it too.

27 June 2017

The other day I developed terrible cold sores around my mouth. They've been hurting like hell for the past couple of days. What is more, they look awful.

At last I overcame my stubbornness and after umpteenth time, finalized my attempts at hiring a tutor to learn Italian and met somebody through Andrea's connections. Despite my cold sores. Her name is Lara. She is quite nice, helpful and kind. Such that she has asked for a small contribution for the lessons because she knows I'm not a local.

When we met we tried to speak in Italian to determine my level. She also asked me if I had any friends here. I did. Although, I wasn't sure if they would be called friends or acquaintances. I was thinking of how to answer that, she interrupted and repeated the same question in English. Well, I was only thinking. I knew my answer in Italian but didn't realize I wasted time thinking about how to put it correct so it sounded less embarrassing that I had only a few buddies.

The intensity of loneliness in my homeland is not the same as in another environment. Whatever I do, I can't hold it as one complete thing, is it always fragmented and it sinks. If it doesn't get fragmented, then I crumble and become aggravating. I reflect on my fight as a reaction to them. As for having no one to hold accountable for my fragments, it is sometimes fine, not so good at other times…

***

I have immense sensitivity toward connection, commitment or having plans made about attachment. In my case, this attachment is realized in an act of disappearance. In other words: ghosting people. I run away because I can't find any solution to the pressure that dawns on me. I feel nauseous when people ask me anything about the future. And if they add me to their future I feel like I'm losing my mind.

***

My landlord took three paintings from the attic that he uses as a storage and he gave them to me. I hung them around the house. They look fine. I bought a few things for the kitchen. I also bought those incense sticks that you put in a bottle of water and they stay here without doing anything except to smell as if they were flowers.

I wanted to dress my flat as if I constantly hosted guests…

It's not bad actually. I might also buy a stand or a portable wardrobe.

***

Quaffed a couple of beers with Andrea. I've known him for a year. He's one of those people I'm seldomly curious about… Why did he go to Berlin from Bergamo? What type of a man was he when he returned?

I don't have those questions on my mind any more.

28 June 2017

Yesterday afternoon I was lying in bed looking at my toes.

The wind through the open window on my right and opposite assisted me and I started gazing at every corner of the room. Walls, the ceiling, furniture, the cover that labels the chair as brand new, pink felt tip pen, the change I've been saving, my backpack, the chair that is unbelievably mismatched with the desk…

As I put my hands on my chest and witnessed my heart rate to rest I began to notice my eyelids grew heavy.

Not long after that I started hearing a periodic sound in my right ear. Someone was breathing. I opened my eyes. I wanted to bend my right knee, turn to my right and with the support of my right shoulder I wanted to raise myself up off the bed. But, no.

This time I only wanted to turn my head. Not the angle I wanted, no, because the breathing was not coming from the empty pillow next to mine but through somewhere between the headboard and the wall. I got the angle this time and even though I knew I could see it properly I began turning my head. This didn't work, either.

The breathing continued. And I felt my eyes were getting dry. Then I had an image as if my pupils had had a full tour around my head and looked to see what was there in my cross right… What I had heard wasn't anything but the breathing of a sleeping dog with a rich reddish golden coat whose tail was resting on my pillow.

Alright, but why was I unable to move?

Sometimes I am frightened by what my mind could do to me.

1 July 2017

It's all about choices and their timing…

Being in the right place at the right time and opting for the correct thing can carry a person to unimaginable heights.

How happy is the person who has now the chance to equate all this!

Occasionally, it proves impossible to make a choice because of a choice made in the past even if I am in the right place now and all I could do then is to watch.

Annoying…

There was a company I wanted to work for so much, be a part of and contribute. Back in the day, I was employed at another place and I helped a friend of mine get a job at this place whose owner I knew. This place became a place of obsession to work for me… And it didn't happen then.

Afterwards I moved away. When I got back I found that although both parties knew how much I wanted to work there they didn't mind and had reached an agreement among themselves. It was easy to play the strong guy. Easy peasy to have acted as if it didn't affect me… Nobody but I knew how much I hurt when I left them there.

***

I try to ignore what occurs sometimes in the hustle and bustle of life.

There is someone screaming inside of me. Someone who wants to bring the house down, who gets mad when his rights are violated against, who believes he deserves certain things more than others and who wants to have them… He's not easy to be silenced. This bears ill-temper and frustration. With myself, with others…

I understand how and why people become mean. They can't help it… This all starts with backing away from conscience one bit, I know. Then you become a little more selfish. More ravenous and sneaky… Less of a sharer. More hypocritical… I get these people so well.

This sickening worldly order of things and people's attitude that leads to unfair competition causes the rest of the people to play the game in the same way.

However, deep within me there's this boy with his rucksack, looking at the world pass by on his first school day and it is impossible for me to do all of the above when he's still with me…

4 July 2017

I checked to see how good I am with preparing Aperol Spritz yesterday. Today, I tried Campari Spritz. It didn't disappoint me.

I have just made one more. Alcohol calms me down…

I had one of my anger fits early this morning. They happen often these days. After I smashed the laptop my dad bought a year ago, I picked up every broken little piece very calmly. I put them in a bin liner and placed it outside the door.

It's Tuesday. Plastics and metals are collected together.

I don't like slow computers. Their screens freeze. Alert errors cause problems all the time. It gets on my nerves that these machines cause problems when they're supposed to serve us and make our lives easier.

It's in the bin now.

I'm not comfortable about it but still…

7 July 2017

I have to clean my bike as soon as I come home.

I may come home knackered. Miserable. I might have tripped over the bike when riding. Every bone and muscle in my body might ache. But I have to be the one to clean my bikes…

It's tubes must be spotless. I can do the chain and the mirror last but handlebars, tyres, down tube, pedals etc. must be spotless and free from dust.

I don't wash it. I just wipe it with a wet cloth. Then dry it. After I do that I put my bike down and watch it because I love watching clean, shiny bikes. I love them so much that I can wipe clean my friends' bikes as well. I even went ahead and did that.

Once, in Istanbul, we rode our bikes for 150 kilometers and came back to mine. I had cleaned both mine and my friend's bike. I think I washed them both because it was a muddy day.

I don't know how I did it in spite of my exhaustion.

And on another day I had met with a friend at a showroom to have his bike cleaned. He had brought Prosecco with him for me…

I love considerate people.

10 July 2017

In my high-ceilinged old apartment, lit by the sun coming in through every corner throughout the day, I was lying down after lunch dreaming.

The weather is so hot that I had to open all the windows for some air. Tulle curtains dance, windows close and shut themselves in the breeze, sometimes hitting hard to the sills. The worst part is, this happens when I'm just about to drift into sleep… I can't ever fall asleep.

Apart from the engine sounds, all I could hear is limited to birds and crickets. When we think of summer the first comes to mind, I guess, is the sounds the crickets make… It is so, at least for me. Just like the smell of sweet melon or chlorine…

The airflow in the room has got so strong that the curtains on both windows have become big balloons…this reminded me of grandad's house in Izmit where we used to go in summer as kids. It was a fabulous place, very bright, high-ceilinged. There was a huge garden surrounding the house. All sorts of trees, flowers, bugs… Animals were my grandad's hobby; he was a hardworking, nature-loving guy who used to have his eggs from his own chickens. I can't forget the pool he built for ducks…

I have never had strong bonds or healthy dialogues with anyone because when our family; better say extended family, came together, there was no proper conversation but about money, houses or cars.

I liked my grandfather; more or less saw him as a second address to go to in order to ask for money if dad wasn't willing to give me some. So, granddad wasn't anything more than this for me at the time.

Though I now understand he and I had so much in common.

Remembering his house at a moment of peace must indeed be a sign of many things…

Unfortunately, there's no room for boasting about the aspects of growing up in a materialistic extended family. Trying to digest and analyse how impacted I was by all this doesn't help at all while I've been away from them for over a year now and cut off every kind of contact. Time is non-refundable.

I'm only in contact with my parents for now. My cousin is located in Samsun, a cute town on the coast of the Black Sea. She also ran away from the vicious circle of Istanbul and had a family.

I live in Italy and he now lives in a small town in Turkey.

We both went mad.

15 July 2017

I love having people at my house. I love cooking my best for them, having them sleep over in clean bedding, feeding them healthy stuff, lending them my bikes, washing up for them and more…

I am accustomed to sharing. I guess it provides me social power. I had to grow up without the presence of a sibling, when I actually had a sibling, and then I completely lost her. It feels less lonely when I have a lot of people in my house.

Sometimes these guests make me feel like I'm imprisoned in my home. Soon as they realize I'm capable of doing everything they stop helping me and all of a sudden, I find myself in the position of a servant. I give and they demand more. Then all my systems break down. I get mad and start looking for excuses to immediately send the person I invited myself back.

Even if they behave well, I start getting agitated when I see their leftovers. Something they wipe their hands with, a glass unwashed, hair visible on light-colored bathroom tiles…

When I invite them I am famished, I keep insisting on things when they're over. But a day goes by and things start falling apart. I take refuge behind negligible things and excuses.

In truth I am extremely disheartened by someone who is dependent on me to do something. I feel pressured. And I quit the bid I entered in order to relieve the pressure off myself.

The founder of the last company I worked for wanted to have a meeting with me regarding the future. "Let's look for answers to some questions together such as what kind of planning we should make, which path to follow for marketing," he had said. The same evening, I decided to quit work.

What does planning the next few years mean? Am I going to stay here that long? A few more years… Going to the same office, doing the same job, seeing the same people for years… I was scared, felt like I was losing my mind.

It was a nightmare.

7 August 2017

I'm one of those who lose it when there's no direction.

There has to be a destination, a city, a restaurant, a bike showroom…

Something.

I'm waiting for my first book to be published. Before it got published, I started the second one.

While I spent June and July anticipating to start a new job in September or October, all of a sudden, I found myself in front of the screen, and it's August. To top it all, at exactly where I wanted to be. Among my friends, among bikes…

Alright but what'll happen next? OK, so I've started to work. Now, I need some things to hold on to.

When I think about the duration of my stay in Italy, this is my third job. Fourth, if I include my Montenegro adventure in between…

I had left a bicycle frame in Istanbul. I'd better have it brought here. It'll be several months for it to arrive considering the whole process. And the excitement will cheer me up for almost a year.

I will steer clear from private Italian lessons and enrol directly at a school. There is a new program starting in September in which I want to register. I believe I miss the school environment from time to time. With my new job I plan to take root here. Perhaps I'll apply for a master's degree next year. We'll see…

I can't resist trying new things, I go mad if I don't.

3 September 2017

I'm at a café I discovered two months ago. This joint became a Sunday routine for me.

Together with fine weather, its staff commuting to work on their bikes and my pen and paper. I love sitting in this little hideaway tucked in a corner of Bergamo's most popular square. It has a pretty yard. I gaze up at the windows and suddenly find myself right in the sky. At the entrance of the yard it is possible to find fine touches in regard to the café, simplicity, zest, elegance and bikes.

Occasional aroma of fresh roasted coffee leaves me with the same sensation of looking at women in their amazing fragrances passing by me. So I involuntarily divert my looks to the direction of the aroma.

Time flows much much slower when you indulge in life's little delights without any expectations.

***

I'm probably going through the most idle Sunday in my life. I'm not using the term idle in a negative sense. On the contrary, I'm in a terrific serenity.

I'm not sure whether it's the flavor of the coffee or how at ease I feel here, but I imagine myself at my favorite coffee bar, Dört Kadıköy, packed with Istanbul youth, in my hometown right now.

Friendly dialogues with people I did not know help me savor the feeling that I belong to some place. The same thing applies to my workplace. I go to work happy and I'm happy when I get back from work. I believe these were the first four weeks in my life when I commuted to work happy and came back happy. This includes my school and professional life.

***

Yesterday morning I decided to adopt a cat. In fact, this decision has been made quite a while now but it felt hard to put it into action and spend the money I saved for it. Now I have a kitty at home waiting for me, whom I haven't even named yet. It was wonderful in the morning to wake up to a house she's now living in. Now there's one more being in the house who has a beating heart…

***

Feeling less anxious… This must be what the state of things being settled, being on the right track means. Experiencing all this not in a daze, but fully aware, is grand.

I want a dog as well. A dog I can take with me anywhere I go, a real buddy.

I feel my eagerness for an ordinary life escalates as my tarnished soul is mended. Family, kids, cats, dogs, weekend trips, work, such things… To put it simply, regular, ordinary things people do.

25 September 2017

It was April or May…

On a Saturday train to Venice from Bassano del Grappa, I was again in a window double seat facing forward dreaming about things.

It was sunny.

The sun was coming through the clouds, warming my hands and face. In one of those moments as I was fascinated by the blue of the clouds, next door a four-seater was occupied by a woman carrying a black cabin-size bag fashionably in harmony with herself.

A woman I couldn't take my eyes off all along the journey…

***

After placing her bag next to the window, she put her feet on it across from her seat facing backwards.

The first detail about her that caught my eye was her delicate ankles. Considering unreliable weather in Northern Italy, she had dressed rather thinly but smart. The hems of her black trousers couldn't disguise her ankles under the carriage's shifting light. The shape of her immaculate black patent leather shoes displayed her ankles beautifully. With thick soles and burgundy stitches, the not-so-neatly tied shoelaces were barely touching her very fair ankles in the hopes of a tan in summer.

She settled in her seat and took out her book. It was an old book with a flimsy cover. I couldn't see what it was because of its angle. Seeing its aged pages and its own red cloth bookmark, I gathered it was an old edition. From time to time she received notifications on her phone. Several messages later she completely switched it off and focused on her book.

***

She was distracted each time there was an announcement as the train approached a station. That's when our eyes met. Each time we exchanged glances I didn't know what to do. The way I held my hands and arms, my posture, my hair, my sleeves… Each time we looked at one another I tried to calm my nerves struggling to find something to do. It was so grand a feeling, even though I knew we were approaching the end of our journey together I was looking forward to the next stop…

***

A proportionate countenance, strong cheeks, a lucky, shapely nose, clothes in perfect harmony with her accessories, indifference challenging the whole world, a voice oozing femininity and mimics dignifying all of these…

And, oh, glasses…

I was incredibly curious about what went on her mind behind those dark grey frames with half-thick lenses that complemented her round features…

***

She reminded me of a woman I fell in love with several years ago. That moment, in that exact second, from head to toe, I pretended her to be that woman. I told her everything, and did everything to make it work. I couldn't in the past, with myself and my own burden back then. I pretended to hold her so tight, kissed her like never before. I would have loved the woman again as if I had never been hurt by her or hurt her before. Her, the reason I felt all the yearning, all the love and all regrets in the world deep in my veins…

***

During the ticket inspection I was lucky to hear her voice, and when a young couple's kid was trying to walk without support in the aisle, I witnessed her smile. I can still visualize both…

At the fourth stops before the terminal stop she put her book back in her bag. Altered the way her feet positioned and clasped her unpolished dainty hands together on her lap. Closed her eyes…

I closed mine, too.

***

Now I was in the same place with her. In the same parallel, in the same universe, sharing the same dream…

I was kissing, inhaling, touching her, listening to her heart, brushing her hair, picking up cat hair off her jumper, holding her hands just for the sake of holding them.

***

She opened her eyes for a while. She put her dark chestnut hair into a sideway loose bun. This way, she was able to fully place her head in the headrest and kept it there until her stop.

***

There were countless opportunities when I had the chance to introduce myself to her and chat her up. I made no such attempts. Before she took her bag and went to the exit, we both stood up to collect our coats from the overhead space. That was the closest we got to each other. If I had moved half a step closer our shoulders might have touched one another.

I never did.

***

She grabbed her carry-on and hastened to the carriage door. I can't forget that image. She had folded her coat in her arm and was holding her carrier. She put her other hand in her trouser's pocket showing up her shapely figure. She had the air of a tough cookie and was standing there in all her grandeur. Before the station's massive roof interfered with the last rays of the sun, I caught a glimpse of her light hair behind her ear and roots of her hair.

She untied her hair. Took her mobile phone and put it in her purse. Walked out on the platform this time in slow steps. A part of me still wanted to talk to her. In fact, every part of me…

I started walking after her. Each of us went ahead of the other taking turns. We could have easily disappeared among the crowd if we wanted to hurry and take advantage of the gaps. Neither of us did. We sometimes walked side by side. We were almost the same height and whenever she came next to me, in those slight moments, I terribly enjoyed imagining us as a couple. I also tried to even my steps with her…

But I still didn't talk to her.

She walked away.

29 September 2017

I'm at places where there's no sun between the dates 29 and 30 September.

I'm 31, my first book Cloud Factory has just been published.

Aside from the ones I saw at the fairs I visited, this is the first time I'm in a caravan. I'm opening and closing its doors, finding out how cleverly the cabinets are installed and sitting amazed at this couch bed.

It's quite small for all these people but I guess it's also what makes these things so likeable. I'll be staying in a tiny teeny caravan with some guys I've only known for a year. One of them, Andrea, technically is my boss and we'll sleep next to one another. Weird but nice…

Doing such a thing, imagining it, is very difficult from where I come from. Those egos, power struggle and a lot more…

Wouldn't ever let it happen back there.

***

We're here as a team for L'Eroica. Arrived here from Bergamo in a four to five-hour ride and we're going back Sunday evening after the races. Each time I come back to Tuscany I get sentimental. My first overseas trip was to Siena. I was walking about the streets today and saw a road sign for Siena which is 27 kilometres away. Perhaps I should call Siena my second home. I am so convinced that one day I will go back there and open the door of my own house…

Just like how sure I am of what my own feelings will be tomorrow and the day after that when I come across Tuscany's picturesque settings…

A magnanimous peace, unique serenity… Tuscany, in the shape of an adoring father figure and a mother's compassion in picking up her child each time he falls…

It embraces you, holds you in and never lets go.

***

The whole team is sleeping together as a matter of fact. It doesn't bother me. My only wish is not being woken up in the middle of the night by snoring chaps.

***

I am spending the day with Andrea. He has given me his friendship and a job. Especially here, in Tuscany… Everything is so magical I don't want it to end. I feel like everything is getting better. In essence, I'm not talking about absolute happiness. I only want the number of days I feel happy a year to increase.

That's all.

30 September 2017

It's seven in the evening. It's been a day of foul nourishment, dirt and fatigue. I didn't want to shower.

It's cold. Maybe I'll have one tonight. I'm in a bad mood and weary. I get like this if I didn't get enough sleep. We rode a total of 50 kilometers today, having gone to Siena and back. I went back to the street where I used to live. Walked about and took a silly shot of myself in front of my old house.

The shutters have been painted. I didn't like the new color.

Last night when the caravan parked in front of the office I was overjoyed. I felt like a kid who was moving into a new house, going into his new bedroom. I'm not as motivated to experience something new, as a kid though.

I've made silly purchases recently; not very happy about it. It's nerve wracking that I waste my resources like this while, in my head, all sorts of things clash with one another. Each time I question or dig deep into things something always comes up to annoy me.

For the same reason, I don't argue with anyone anymore. Conflict tires me out. My longing for a quiet and stable life has intensified recently... I don't even want to travel to Taiwan. I wish the trip was canceled. The moments I come home from work and pet my cat are the ones I desire most. Thinking of such things, dreams of relocating less is desirable. I want to live in perpetuity. That sounds more feasible to me these days.

***

There are just too many people around me. It's really jam-packed here. Lots of people gathered together in the same place, for the same purpose... I feel pressure. I don't want to do things out of obligation. When I go through such a period, I get a strange feeling that I'm missing out on some other stuff.

Now that it's not possible to exist in more than one location, it'll be much sane for me to be exactly where I want to be. Do what exactly I want to do. After all, there's no end to aspiring to do different things and being elsewhere. Endless imagination... I can be in a mood to continually desire, get carried away by dreams. That ruins my days: constantly wanting or craving other stuff.

It's not reasonable to swim in these waters. It's deep. There's a high probability of drowning.

1 October 2017

I couldn't get enough sleep again. I indulged in booze at dinner. As I wanted to get trashed, I drank one after the other but couldn't get a deep sleep. When I woke up my nose was burning up. It must be a sign that I'll get sick. All members of the Stelbel team are on their way. Andrea is right behind them on his motorbike. My coffee isn't strong enough…

I feel completely alienated against everything that is going on around me. All these people, their actions, what they talk and laugh about…

I want to dispatch myself from this ambiance that I don't feel the slightest part of and go back home.

The only sound I hear is noise. Random, out of tune, grey noise…

***

Photographs and writings are my essentials. They make me feel better when I'm troubled. In fact, when I create something that trouble disappears. In order for certain things to keep flowing creating is a must.

6 October 2017

I'm in my favorite transportation vehicle.

I put my feet up on the opposite seat.

On my way to Milano on the last scheduled train.

***

It wasn't only my loved ones that I had left behind when I departed my homeland, the city I was born in. A great more recollection of things I didn't like were left behind along with them as well. I leave my persky posts with their scraped off paints behind the window.

But we tend to favor only the peachy moments in our lives and their painful residue. Our culture teaches us to worship drama and agony.

On the contrary, there's a lot more that we dislike and do not ever want to see again…

All those people, all that's happened, all the places, all those smells…

All that is not supposed to happen.

16 October 2017

I'm about to fly to Taiwan from South Korea on an A350-900.

I'm a little heartbroken by what I observed during the flight from Milano and what I witnessed here at the airport. I flew 11 hours from Europe. All those hours and continents…

What I've encountered after I landed is exactly the same as before.

Technology-addicted mutants. Another form of stereotyping… The sum of actions of all diverse people is now called globalization and someone is making an obscene amount of money on this.

18 October 2017

We started at 7.37 in the morning, from Taipei, we're off to the city where the race will take place.

Yesterday was the first day I fully spent in this city. It's a populous city. Just like any other metropolis, it is disorderly. These types of cities usually change a person. I didn't observe these qualities in this city.

Dishonesty and intolerance are not to be found here as in similar metropolises. People are in a rush. Perhaps even stressed out, too… However, they don't use these as an excuse to bother others.

The same applies both to evenings and days. White collars and those who go out at night, they both behave the same…

The city is not a beautiful one. It's full of high rises, lots of grey, not-so-creative billboards, shop signs mismatched with their buildings, etc.

That's all I report for the time being about a city that rain clouds never leave.

22 October 2017

I'm waiting for my first outbound flight at Taipei Airport.

I couldn't not exactly produce a precise answer if I were asked about my expectations. In brief, it just wasn't a trip I was expecting. I'm too knackered to go into any detail about it.

What I feel among all these lined-up lounge seats is loneliness and failure.

***

I've missed my cat so much but I don't fancy returns. I wish that everything was about nothing but departures… Or, if only I could find an excuse to turn each trip into a succession of departures and that way, I could motivate myself…

***

I'm as much alone in my destinations as I am where I live…

It echoes one of my ex-girlfriend's words, "Gökhan you are going to die alone."

31 October 2017

For quite some time I haven't had anyone but Zelda in my life..

I don't talk to anyone except for forced chats that I meet through momentary meet-ups.

And I become more sluggish after solitary dinners…

My loneliness has now divided into two: before dinner and after dinner.

Sometimes I suffer. Then it fades away.

For a brief moment…

6 November 2017

Some smells remind me of home.

Recognizable scents prevail in the rooms that remain pretty much untouched back home. It is hard not to associate smells with home.

But not impossible. We can find associations...

***

I didn't imagine these would be the thoughts going through my mind as I left my house this morning. With my glum face, I stepped into the office. Tranquility is possible, even in small amounts, because the smell that welcomed me in the office also made me smile. I felt as if I had returned to where I belonged.

So peculiar, but, ah yes, it was serene.

13 November 2017

My love, all those that I love, my brotherly mates, and many others who are close to me…

If I am far away, so are all of them.

They are neither present in my favorite tune nor at the other end of the phone line when I need them the most…

Even though they never got as ugly as to question me, "Did you consult me when you were leaving?" They keep reminding me that I am desolate at every opportunity or occasion I ever need them.

Well, I took the risk of fleeing from my homeland and now I should be prepared for this.

Isn't that so, Gökhan?

Not at all…

Unfortunately, anticipating something and confronting it doesn't have the same impact…

If that were the case would a potential mother be on cloud nine?

Or would a girl run exhilarated towards her parents knowing her exams were a success?

Reality makes itself visible when it hits me. And, loneliness forces itself onto me when reality knocks at my door…

I start listening to my favorite songs on my own. It reminds me of my loneliness.

***

I used to think on school busses at elementary school…

I would ask myself, "how?"… How come everyone I see, talk to or touch has their own lives…

Was the world so big? Was there enough capacity for everyone? Was there enough space on these streets for everyone so they could cherish long lives?

Some mornings I wake up with this realization. Over and over again ... Almost everything that moves when I see through my window has a life and - of course - a story. The people in the travel photos I look at, and the person who takes the shot of them ...

Everyone!

Incredible...

18 November 2017

I'm so lonely it hurts now.

Sometimes I get tears in my eyes within an instant. Like kids who get their fingers stuck in a door. For no reason at all, all of a sudden…

I grind my teeth so I don't cry. I try to pull myself together annoyed that I act like a headstrong child who stumbles. Sometimes I succeed. Often, I don't.

Sometimes it becomes impassable to hold back the tears. When that happens, my cat comes over and lays on my chest, looks at me, makes me laugh a bit. She then starts licking me on the cheeks with her pink, sandpaper-like tongue.

I surrender, of course, as there's no one else joining me...

***

I'm neither there nor here… I've never been able to manage a steady rhythm in any of the packs. I joined; but, I've always kept solo. Wherever I infiltrated, the same thing happened.

This situation did not make a difference for my bike, either.

I had a few friends here. Then I became their colleagues. But, their world is connected through a different thread to my world of bikes… They're fast, they perform well, they can ride longer and they can handle cold better. They talk of bikes more. So much that sometimes they talk about nothing else. They constantly ride together and they no longer want me beside them. I can't blame them. I like taking long, lasting, cherished looks at the places I ride through. And them… they like to accelerate…

In these circumstances my loneliness deepens. It has intensified so much and I do not know what to do, more importantly, where to go.

Would I be defeated if I returned to the land I came from? Or would there still be hope for me in some other lands?

Every person gets tested in some way or another. I believe I am being tested with walkaways… With not being able to stick around… With not being able to mingle, become a 'part ofs'…

***

Apart from battling with all that, there is another aspect: my mind. I'm so lonely. I keep brooding. Keep fretting about. I talk to myself as there's nothing better to do but my loneliness doesn't subside for one second. I can't remember the last time someone invited me to a place.

***

There are times that I hesitate to check my phone. Because I don't want to wonder and see where they went this time…

I get too tired of and stressed out by thinking where they went, what they have eaten. From time to time I can't resist and check. Just like I did a minute ago.

It's seven in the evening. They went to grab something to eat after their ride, all sweaty in their outfits. I ask myself, if I would prefer to do this.

Would I have spent the whole day on a bike as if I had no purpose, no life at all…

Would I have lived like this on days I didn't work?

***

Some answers to the questions change depending on the time they get answered.

It's upsetting not to socialize. Combined with melancholy, this pressure compels me to look at their photos and then knocks me over. However, in good times it would never even be on my agenda.

Perhaps these people are not cut out for me.

I haven't met people whom I would relate more to, to have substantial friendships. I don't know…

Am I being too hard on myself?

Is everything unwittingly more dramatized when you're alone?

19 November 2017

I think of myself as a clock. Nine o'clock.

I am exactly at 12 o'clock. My back is against the pillows which is against the bedrest, my knees are slightly bent…

My red bike is at 3 o'clock. It's the reason why I often keep turning my head left… The colorful one is at 6 o'clock. Directly opposite from me; the least I communicate with but the most I'm ensured of its existence…

At nine o'clock is my white bike. The last stop before me, foul weather friend…

But there's something wrong with this clock. Even if every part of it is well located time is not passing.

***

Anyway, there has never been a sign since my childhood as to whether I am good for anything. Anyone.

My concern is how far I can go by myself.

29 November 2017

So far I've never encountered anything positive that meets the eye at immigration offices in Italy. Whether they're government buildings or NGO's, they all provide their services in dingy places. Lots of immigrants, mostly Africans, waiting in line for their turns, and in return, only a bunch of people trying to serve them properly…

The clerk's attitude is generally tired and fed up. Maybe due to work load or maybe they're prejudiced against immigrants…

For adults with kids it is quite sad that no allowances were made in cold waiting lounges.

I can only set CGIL, a union-like entity, aside. At least they have tried to turn that stuffy cell down in the gutter. Into a bearable place for kids with its small tables, matching chairs and not-so matching toys of many colors in a plastic box…. Depending on which perception one adopts, this situation might be defined as alright.

But still, it is pretty hard to talk about niceties or happiness in a place of no mobile phone coverage.

***

There are innumerable notices on the bulletin board. All of them are instructions and refer to major documentation in order to finalize certain procedures. Only in Italian though. It is in a clear tone, sentences are short and what it says is open to comments.

"Are you thinking about going back home?" The inscription is much bigger than the others. It's colored, looks cuter and translated into five different languages.

7 December 2017

I'm inspired to write in the most inconvenient places.

It's while I'm off to lunch with colleagues, riding my bike to work in the morning or while I'm at home doing literally nothing…

***

This morning on my way to work, I thought how many more times I would have to, or would, pass the same street. How many more times will it take to finish? At what speed would I have to ride for it to come to a finish? What kind of thoughts should I be thinking on the way so it's more bearable?

2018 will soon arrive. What, for example, in the new year, if I passed the street on each work day would this journey finish more quickly? 100, 200, 300… What if I passed it every waking day?

How many times should I pass the same speed bumps? How many more times should I meet other bikers' gazes? How many more times should I bicker?

Does the road come to an end? Or am I the only one who winds up drained as I pass the same road…

Sure, I have a few guesses but nowadays I'm in such a foul mood I'm unable to trust the voices that my mind composes. It's not clear where they're coming from or what they're saying. Some sound like they come out my own voice. I'm not convinced whether they are quite deep. They sound like they're coming from elsewhere and from unparalleled moods.

***

On my way to work my gaze is caught up in vast greenery that seems infinite. It is not bounded by a mountain or a small hill. Vast, flat greenery that lies ahead all the way to the horizon…

I walk to that vanishing line wearing my backpack… I very much belong to that infinitely beautiful scenery… My soul permeates right there… I imagine being comfortable and warm. Even though I am shivering.

***

The more I am in places I don't want to be at, the more I become the person I don't want to be. The more I smell like I don't want to smell, the more I seem to others in a way I don't want to seem. I see more of the things I don't want to see. I inject more data into my brain that I don't need to hear. It is a waste in every aspect, waste of time and loneliness…

***

My soul is so inclined to certain stimulants, even more so alien to some others though it was formerly exposed to them… Charming lights, some tunes, cobblestones slipping away underneath my feet, a few smiling faces and a lot more that's lined up…

9 December 2017

The air is crisp but glistening…

The sun was whirling around the house. I cleaned the house instead. I didn't want to watch more of how the dust particles danced in the air highlighted by the sun coming in through the window.

I threw away all the stuff that I could grab.

There were a few items I had been keeping. I dreamt of a house and a family of my own.

Also threw away some keepsakes from the first bike race that I took part in, and L'Eroica, several months after that… Threw them all away. I used to think I would keep my race gear and racer number and have them framed.

It appears that none of that matters.

10 December 2017

I haven't set foot outside in two days.

Except for the orange peels I chucked away in XL size garbage bags parked right outside my door…

I realized I hadn't looked out of the window in two days. I heard kids screaming outside. When I responded to my cat, and had to clear my throat to speak, he kept looking at me and meowed.

The scene outside was well worth looking at and smiling for one second.

It's snowing in Bergamo…

Each snowdrop was the equal size of a piece of plush carpet in my bedroom. The snow had already started filling the street, the gardens between my street and the old city and parked cars all white.

I hope it doesn't last long. If it does, each second that I'm witnessing kids' fun my test against loneliness will become twice as hard to overcome.

Anyway, who would play snowball with me?

28 December 2017

I'm in Milano. I've missed enjoying the feeling of being a tourist in big cities.

I've never used the underground network in this city before as I had always taken my bike along. This time I didn't. Stops, interchange stations, color-coded underground stations... Moving under the ground in other cities as if solving puzzles. An occasionally melancholic puzzle, shifting around without knowing what's expecting you over the ground...

How about the Paris metro, imagine when you're caught up on the Paris metro network... Life is utterly different in those cities. Multi-layered metro stations where you witness people of all kinds and their strangeness along with others who look like they've been put there by hand, all mute and rigid, bereft... They never move until the approaching train chugs and they're hit by the whiff of dampness in the air.

31 December 2017

The only thing on my mind during the final week of the year was to go to Florence. You know what they say; how you see the new year defines what the new year will be like for you…

***

I stay in bed when I can't find the motivation to live. My cat, my laptop and a few cookies…

Today was one of those days.

Wanting to go to Florence wasn't sufficient by itself to plan the trip. On the other hand, I wasn't in a state to greet the new year in Bergamo, either. The past year was fine but Bergamo doesn't offer anything further.

That's why I'm writing this on a train to Venice. It was around two in the afternoon when I purchased the tickets. I would like to return early tomorrow morning because I'm not willing to leave my cat alone for a long time. She misses me. And I miss her… She doesn't have anybody but me.

I don't either…

6 January 2018

I do not know how I look from there. I guess I'm more hunched than before… It feels like I bend my head more as I walk. As if I'm hardly carrying my own brain… My frame is angled forward and I strenuously raise my head. It's gotten burdensome to raise my head and look ahead.

I only see my steps now.

***

I am ghostlike in all the places I go. A silent ghost who goes to work, goes shopping, feeds himself, pets his cat from time to time.

It is contrary to reason to exist as nothing but a ghost, while my mind searches for clues to thousands of ruminations in the midst of poor nutrition.

Sometimes the pain in my front lobe is unbearable. It's as if those thousands of ruminations knocked a huge pine tree over, held it at both ends and banged it on the front of my head. Harder at each time… In doing so, they've vigorously held on to the imaginations of rejoining the places they'd dreamed of. And the worst part is, there are no contradictory ruminations which will say no to them…

***

I apologized to one of my old mates. Our friendship had fallen apart and I wanted to start the year anew, mend things. His presence was always a support to me, a valuable person…

We made up now.

***

I have a feeling that I will not be in Bergamo next year.

I've been looking into flats in Como and Florence recently. I intend to flat-share and live like that for a while. I need some tranquility within the limits of books, photography and bikes.

I have to live without receiving instructions from anyone. And I don't want much obligation either. I do not have a target to become a renaissance man. It'll be enough if what I touch is warmly welcomed by myself and by the people who cherish them…

12 January 2018

The clock shows 10pm… I am on a plane.

I am reading the "Use me if you feel sick" sign on the brown bag in front of me.

I immediately moved away from the Spanish couple next to me as soon as I spotted a vacant window seat. I don't like people who have zero personal space. Essentially, the whole aircraft itself is bothersome to me… It flies. But also destroys the magic of traveling. Travelling is more to do with trains and coaches if you ask me…

Of which the world goes by behind its windows, in which you move slowly and cherish the journey...

Airplanes are the final stages of the journeys. Like the goals scored in football games. You watch the marvelous passes, the midfield, tactical line-up, then goal and the festival is over. It's the same with flying. Bang! You're there. There are no opportunities present for one to see what others are doing on earth apart from take-off and landing. Majority of the time there are clouds, a bit of a sun over there, sometimes snow-covered summits… If we're lucky. Sometimes there's only darkness…

***

I completed my sixth month in my latest job in Italy. The three of us, Andrea, Alessandro and myself had a meeting over half an hour because they'd kept thinking of what we achieved in six months and what we could do in the coming months. This time I didn't feel nauseous or didn't invision to quit.

They're pleased with me. As they were saying, "It would be good if you did that. Actually, let's put you in charge of this, too! You're good at this, as well," I didn't realize how time went.

But, I certainly noted some items in my shit list…

"If we don't express anything negative or warn you, we are happy with what you're doing."

Right.

The thin line between leadership and management has become so noticeable in that moment that I suddenly fell off one of the cracks. I felt the right and wrong running in my blood…

I didn't assess this either as an appraisal or approval. If it had been merely self-indulgent, I believe, I still wouldn't have wanted to write about this a day later.

I can't digest this.

It really disheartens me that people are so shallow, square and tremendously indifferent to the happiness of their employees.

23 February 2018

I have never been the person that people I cared about wanted me to be. I was never able to be present in their space; close enough to be hugged each time they wanted to; nor was I endured enough to grant them the peace they required of me when we woke up under the same roof.

Sometimes I suspect I am the sole benefactor of the decisions I made. Things I carried out as a consequence. I am not sure if this is what it has to be. It seems there is a cliff between the situations I invest in or witness during the day and the way I am, the personality I possess.

***

I sometimes meet Zelda's gaze. I take one last look at myself in the mirror as I'm about to leave my serene home.

"Don't go," she says. "Stay, let's chill together. Never mind work. Stay and write, I won't be a hassle."

***

Sometimes I'm too big for my life. And, at other times, I can't fill the voids much as I reach out to them…

25 February 2018

Will all the waiters' smiles or better still, friendly dialogues at my usual restaurant make me feel like I belong here, in Bergamo? Is there a direct association of getting close to becoming a native of a place, to the number of people you know or in contact with in that place?

***

They've got used to seeing me alone here… They don't ask, "Table for one?" any longer. They know I like dessert after my course. That I ask for coffee just as I'm finishing dessert, as well… They still have difficulty pronouncing my name but they all know me much better than many women whose lips spilled my name. Or my friends, who already know a lot about me… Perhaps it's because they can empathize… Perhaps they were not raised as self-centered, selfish individuals… Or maybe, it's because I pay them…

***

I'm scribbling this on the back of a piece of paper ripped off the menu of delicious starters at Da Mimmo's. It was no trouble to obtain a pen and this paper. Maybe it's because I'm approachable or maybe I'm their regular customer…

***

The restaurant I regularly eat at, my favorite barber, the mountain I enjoy most to climb, the brunette who delivers my food shopping, mountain bike enthusiast boy, the roads I like walking, the streets I adore, the store I favor its employees, that little café that I fancy being able to drink coffee at all times, the ice cream seller who notices my Italian has improved…

They all belong to me either long-term or short-term. But I don't belong to them.

Not in the least.

What one must do in order to belong to a city, an identity, to a woman, a family or to a job? Stretch the timeline he spends there? Or pretend he is someone else? I really don't know.

At all.

10 June 2018

Quest is the essence of existence...

That godforsaken quest for meaning that picks our brains and never leaves some of our minds, as we, in all boorishness, go through the lives granted to us without knowing how and why, only because the sun rises every morning...

***

There is not much that has made me forget where I have been, turned a deaf ear to and even has blinded me. It can't be said that I take pleasure in ambition for success, access to money or anything alike. These are not the sort of things that satisfy one when one has acquired them. More is always available. It is always possible to aim higher. To lose oneself with greed, shaken with ambition, to be so blinded that you can't perceive what's ahead of you, and successive fits of anger... All of these trigger one another and imprison a person, and makes him/her a part of an awful cycle of events.

***

I came across the one thing that enabled me to realize I was devoid of the breath. I took it as I closed my eyes...

Love.

I live for love. It has contributed to my life as long as it has existed. The love that, merged with a trifling reminiscence, could take me back to years as if I got on a simple boat and sailed toward an endless blue horizon. The love that could lift me up only to mercilessly push me down so it could watch me fall. Well, that presence is more like a boogie broadcast that appears on tv screens in villages between two countries. Still, her short longevity is more than enough to make me happy.

It's as if everything is for all of this...

All those roads, all those women, all those photos, my hills, the summits I went on, going out on the street on the spur of the moment to watch midnight snow, my cats, goats I fed by hand on one of the islets near Kekova, a small island in the southern regions of Turkey, my drinkings, my getting losts, my dreams, the hearts I broke… I, myself, who cannot go any further than getting aggressive when things don't work out, even if I wanted to give life a meaning.

It is love.

***

My character likes finding 'another new' with growing curiosity. Thus, testing myself with a more herculean task… Running away from every place, every undertaking, and ultimately, every person who makes you feel like you keep going around in circles.

Or when love comes to me, will I ruin it? OR will I find myself caught up in something that will never fade away?

17 June 2018

I still couldn't jump off the huge swing we rode on together in Brussels and yet you did.

I'm still in swing…

I sometimes accelerate swinging because I get tense. Then I visualize your face and my anger subsides. Though sometimes I want to ride as high as I can and reach that certain point that nobody has reached. The highest point ever, where I will squint against the sun…

Perhaps only then will I see you again. You will appear in the next swing all of a sudden…

You will welcome me again with open arms, a cynical smile on your face…

1 July 2018

I came to Turkey; I'll just take a look.

I had to weigh how I'd feel on its streets, see what the visual feast on its southern coast would mean to me, observe my understanding while I was with my own people.

The result was a huge blow.

***

I walked about my favorite neighborhoods in stillness cherishing the sights. Passed the streets I knew. Got lost in the ones I didn't. Some venues I once had liked to spend time in, shut down. I tried to move quickly when I passed the ruined buildings but I couldn't ignore the ones that stuck out. I was shaken by the sight of an entry-level flat, in spite of all life left behind there; it was a building and the fences around its windows, doors, garden, even the cobbles in the narrow path to the gate were removed. There were many strips of tapes still remaining on the pink walls in the room next to it.

A child's memories dreamily looking at countless posters well-taped on the wall were no longer there as they had flown out of the windows….

Quite similar to our hopes and memories having been ripped apart when my cousin and I saw our apartment building, that warm place in which its gardens we had sown watermelon seeds, did not exist anymore…

We had good times.

3 July 2018

Because of buildings constructed one after the other with no artistic concern, looking like incompatible family members who, very obviously, are cautious of each other when forcibly lined up for special day photos, we now turn not our faces but our backs to the cities we live in…

***

People in Europe reside in places facing the streets closed to traffic, squares as well as historical buildings. Their tables, chairs and usual sitting arrangements are all organized according to this fact. Whereas in Turkey, people turn their back to details. Istanbul offers beauty. People just watch the water. The shades of blue are irresistibly beguiling and there is no problem with the calm the sea offers. However, Turkey's problem is people like me, we thoroughly turn our backs to the cities whose locals we have social conflicts with.

The cities we ignore, turn our backs to, weeps behind us as we watch the Bosphorus while its colors fade…

***

People of Turkey, we nervously ignore each other claiming we have to walk steady and mind our steps.

4 July 2018

My mind is fuzzy.

Fobies I never used to have when I moved to Bergamo from Istanbul stand before me tenaciously. Especially when I want to depart from Bergamo to start another life.

I have collected so much stuff, either tangible or tactable…

***

I call them achievements but I wonder if these achievements turn out to be my burdens? Is it because of my achievements that I'm unable to shift my position?

How about, if there is a lot that accumulates only to be lost in the end, how much of this achievement is a gain?

10 July 2018

This morning I decided what kind of a house I want to live in.

A well-lighted house, where I wake up to birds singing each morning, where, in its room, I spend much of my time and see many shades of green, and its walls, full of frames…

I do not know where to locate this house.

I only have the image of the house for now.

***

It has to be such a room that it will take up all my time…

I have to open my eyes there in the mornings… Make love and get drunk with my lover… Smell of flowers should prolong the room when I open the window in the middle of the night for cool air, the earthy scent should fill my lungs each morning…

12 August 2018

When I left my house this morning birds as well were asleep.

Only crucial stuff in my backpack, the better part of a little, in my pocket and questions on my mind, taking a break...

***

Every airport is identical to the other... Including this one, as well as the sensation they radiate.

I leave as if I'm running away, following huge arrows. What other walkaways are so smooth as this?

If only we were always shown the direction we were supposed to go... If only I could know what would happen if I went in that direction. Or, this, the direction of the blue arrow...

***

Two tall women are strolling down in front of me, feet inward, hunched under the heavy bags. They're window shopping with an air of getting dragged by their feet, unkempt hair, tattooed arms, canvas shoes.

Now and then we move forward only because we are obliged to. Maybe always... When there's all that goodness for keeping still, life interferes with everything, screaming at us, "I'm here!"

Alright, you're there but how many of us are there with you? How many of us really want to go to that place you want to take us to? How many of us really want to move forward with you and witness what your surprises are?

***

I would like to slowly move farther away from the modern world in certain cities. I wish...

The buildings I leave behind as I come out of the train station suddenly disappeared, the people walking before me shrank, roads made of asphalt were turned back into their original forms and even replaced with cobblestones. I wish sidewalks and bike paths were transformed into soil. I wish I saw pedestrians all dressed up, workers in rubber wellies covered in mud as slow riding horse carriages...

As I walk carelessly toward the city center, I am thinking about new destinations.

***

Insistent beggars appeared late at night by my side, made me go through moments that I hadn't had in ages. Moments I knew well but had forgotten...

They made their presence known without any respect. The smell of their breath, their stench and bloodshed eyes ended my drowsiness. While I was waiting for the red tram, which also brings a lot of fresh memories from the previous stops. These beggars were so disturbing. I had to leave my seat.

Once again, I've come to realize the immense damage metropolises cause. At the same time, I was overjoyed by the fact that spending over two years in Bergamo, I was able to erase my habits of at least twenty years gained in my past life in Istanbul...

13 August 2018

The tramway, once giving you the impression that you're sliding on tracks, is not so kind to those who are not on it.

First you hear its hum, its shake. I, too lazy to clean the gums in my eyes, cannot resist the tram. Somehow hearing it arrive sounds like a lullaby I'd hear in a crib. I stay in bed a little longer…

***

I have to be at places that inspire me in order to have a good relationship with myself. Spending time with myself means introspection, tending to things that I enjoy or revisiting them. It's more like sifting through lentils, the things that my fingertips touch…

How far can I go away from myself when each new surrounding takes me back to another memory in another chapter in my life?

***

I eagerly grab my pen with no knowledge of what to write about and then I freeze like a child who stops before he sneezes, squints and covers his mouth.

If only he sneezed; he'd be free, and so would I…

***

I collected heaps of memories in my palms touching this velvet couch when it was new. I was curious to know how it would feel. Yes, under these high ceilings supported by thick columns that have marble patterns on them, which I watch with interest, all of which make me feel small and insignificant…

As I pop in and out of historical cafes in Vienna, which modestly welcome the decent attitude of their locals who are at peace with themselves, I sense a strange enchantment in each of my steps, in every move, toward the lives before me.

I believe I drift more away from loneliness in each new city…

When I travel, the river I swim in flows in the same direction with me. I distance away from the damp stench. Everywhere smells fresh, of the new, of the sea and of grass. My strokes are faster now. Once I get there; I will not let them become me, I will embrace those smells with the same eagerness; as if for the first time, each time, at each attempt…

"I wish I could get there…" I keep saying. "I wish I could get there!"

Again, from the start, frightened that I will arrive again in loneliness…

14 August 2018

There has been no other city that I was less bothered by rain. I've been walking under the grey sky all morning. I neither care about how wet I got. For how long the raindrops fall down?

I'm observing the people and the landscape while I'm getting soaked.

***

Off to Bratislava, the small city that I'm unsure of the duration of stay. Happy windmills and doubtful clouds assist me… I love them, even behind the bus window.

***

Overlooking the old city from the top, whilst its tiles are being renewed, among the tower's monumental walls, there is also a back garden, so green, stretched out in the field.

Before I know it, we're two people sitting on the walls as I watch part the Danube and part the garden. Perhaps I wouldn't have stayed that long here if it weren't for the pretty Asian woman who sat next to me. She was wearing a dress that made her look very elegant, shades of mélange scattered on a few other tones, a small black clutch with thin straps held across her body between her visible shoulder blades and white shoes.

I wouldn't have gone on the swing. I wouldn't have sat under the tree uncomfortably and wouldn't have dreamed. If it weren't for her.

***

Too tiny but busy enough to be a capital city, I loved Bratislava's Tuesday noise and landscape.

Just as I say to myself "It's finished, that's it," a new street and a new corner emerges and it tires me, without realizing it.

But it's worth every step I take.

I did want someone next to me in this city…

I'm convinced Bratislava would become more brilliant than it already is with a group of good friends or with someone I never met but who lives here.

It would have been wonderful to casually spend time around the streets hemmed in by great walls that surround not only the castle but the city, as well for a few days. Had I not been so lonely.

I walked on the streets besieged by restaurants, not minding the small stones that got into the poor soles of my cheap shoes. I slowed down in narrow streets spreading my arms. Stood standing a fair amount of time in the square.

I watched kids play in the paddling pool. Sat on the steps of house doors I liked. Took shitty photos.

I did this all alone.

I have social-anxiety. Nevertheless, I wish somebody showed me around, then the next minute, I don't stop whining. When I don't know what I really want, I also can't stand my own self.

***

Bratislava's colorful buildings reminded me of a box of chocolate mixes that guests used to bring back in Turkey. I used to love some of those chocolates; each individually wrapped and in different colors. But some, I would have a bite and chuck away.

There are some buildings that leave you speechless.. Just admiring them for minutes… It is not possible to say the same thing for some others. They look for their admirers, stand quite lonely in their pale yet unpopular colors.

15 August 2018

Am I acting appropriate to time's arrow? Am I being disrespectful to the spirit of this place by sitting with my laptop here? This place used to host files, binders, typewriters and ink stains.

Waking up in Vienna is formidable.

So is being here, writing on this marble desk.

23 November 2018

I've just hung up the phone.

I was talking to my dad. My father, whose birthday was today, with whom I could never have a working relationship…

***

I kept thinking about my dad all day long. A few memories came to mind that never did before.

One of them involved a drawing for my projects. At middle school, we sometimes had homework assignments for the art class and we drew the instructions at home and then submitted them in class. However, I was not talented enough to draw or paint. Therefore, I either didn't do my assignments or, if my father was in a good mood, I would ask him to do them for me.

Once we were asked to draw an animal in black pencil. What first occurred to me was to draw the animal in one go but after several attempts I had given up. Compelled to submit the assignment, I asked my dad who had come home happy and started watching him draw. In no time, the lion's head appeared with its proud stance and I was flabbergasted. I, thinking quite systematically, had only focused on drawing the whole animal. Whereas my dad was able to finish the portrait of a lion in a few minutes. Noticing how surprised I was, my dad had said, "If you understand it is a lion when you look at it, then there's no problem," and got up and left. He just didn't realize he had left a son admiringly looking at him from behind.

***

On a different occasion, as I was untalented in pastel painting as well as drawing, I tried to find a solution to my problem again. I took a yellow box of MonAmi paints, then a very reputed brand, and went up to my dad.

This time the assignment was a thick forest and mountains behind it. After many failed attempts my hands were covered in paint. I pushed the box of paints toward my dad, he took only what he needed and first started by lightly drawing and then coloring them in. The result was again fantastic. Huge pine trees with noticeable brown bodies and mountains in dark brown and grey with their rugged surfaces, all so visible to the eye…

***

It appears I had to spend several years away from my dad. He always held an artist's melancholy. In fact, we had many common grounds…

20 January 2019

I'm not sure which reality I should cling to?

Which one is my own reality?

Is it the never-ending urgent tasks at the office? Corners of the enormous world yet waiting to be discovered? My unzippable and fully packed backpack? All those people I met when I traveled to Istanbul to see the play adapted by my first book? Coffee I had with Cem Seymen the next day? The aspects I attach to my own self from the book I read? The future of my children, if I should have a family? Family? Or my loves, the women in my life?

Which one is my own reality?

3 February 2019

Today I put the final touches on my second book.

More interestingly, the British guy, now unemployed, was also at my house to catsit Zelda when I'd be flying to Istanbul for my birthday. In short, I was able to focus on the thing I wanted to finish while there was somebody else in the house to distract me. This is a big progress for someone like me who

is a procrastinator.

***

Each time I visit Istanbul, the city I was born and brought up in, I find it more complicated and challenging than my previous visit. It's either that I'm losing my habits to live in a metropolis or Istanbul is getting intolerable day by day.

I wish I could find a way to rip my family away from there. I keep insisting that they should move to the south, I keep telling them of the advantages of living a healthier and more quiet life. At the same time, I am in total understanding of how hard it might be to sell your property and buy another one in another location after a certain age.

***

It was a pure nourishment for my soul to be with people that I had missed and enjoy the most beautiful corners of the city within a limited time.

Burak was one of those people. He was a little pensive but things seem to be working alright for him. Even though marriage is a whole new thing for him, he's managed it well. I could say it's still a nightmare to me.

I also wanted to meet with Onur before I departed but there was no time. He's in the departures section, wants to leave Turkey as well. It's the best action to take in order to offer a better life for his wife and child.

***

As for the people of Istanbul, they're still the same... Most of the population is aggressive, inclined to run over each other on the street, disrespectful, intolerant and self-centered... They're not any different outside or on social media...

Too bad.

I'm so reluctant to return. In all of my nightmares, I see myself back in Istanbul. Just like the first few nights after I completed my military service, I kept having nightmares about being very frightened to go back, being made to go back...

***

I achieved many things that I wasn't able to before...

I finished writing two books to say the least. I learned to cook a lot of dishes, not to get sick, to be self-sufficient and not to bite my nails. I even started pilates to fix my hunched posture. I understood how important self-discipline is in order to keep things at a working order. Otherwise, it would be impossible to advance my Italian and work at the same office. It's easy to say, but I've been working at the same office for 18 months. I take better care of my cat now. Zelda never got sick so far. However, both Siena and Niccolò had gotten seriously ill twice.

***

I'm about to complete my third year in Bergamo. I feel I've started to peel off my supranational identity of being an immigrant. I'm entering my own home when I come to Bergamo. My towels, my bed, the couch I sit on, the smell in my wardrobe... They all belong to me.

I know, I'm going to leave here, too. Days will come when I'll feel stonewalled and I will again hit the road for some other culture...

But, that's okay! That's life...

Ever flowing, feeling others, something that completely destroys plans, similar to removing a block in Jenga... Something destroyed, scattered, dissolved, blown out but, essentially, something that's been slipped into our hands to rebuild.

www.ingramcontent.com/pod-product-compliance
Lightning Source LLC
Chambersburg PA
CBHW072043160426
43197CB00014B/2611